A Thief in the Night

A Thief in the Night

Unraveling the Mystery of Technology, Prophecy, and Christ's Return

By
Lee Kedrie

A Thief in the Night. Copyright © 2005 by Lee Kedrie. All rights reserved.

Cover illustration copyright © 2005 by Lee Kedrie. All rights reserved.

Author's photo copyright © 2005 by Lee Kedrie. All rights reserved.

All rights reserved. This book is protected under the copyright laws of the United States of America. No part of this book may be reproduced in any form or by any electronic or mechanical means including information storage and retrieval systems for commercial gain or profit. The use of short quotations or occasional page copying for personal or group study or literary review is permitted and encouraged. Permission will be granted upon request. All Scripture quotations, unless otherwise indicated, are taken from the Holy Bible New International Version®. NIV®. Copyright © 1973, 1978, 1984 by International Bible Society. Used by permission of Zondervan Publishing House. All rights reserved. Requests for information should be sent to the publisher at:

English Channel Press
P.O. Box 461174
Aurora, Colorado 80046-1174
http://www.englishchannelpress.com
303-699-3383

"Using Technology to Reach the World for Christ"

ISBN: 0-9766307-0-2

Library of Congress Control Number: 2005901600

Edited by Barb Spitz and Mary Lou McGinnis
Cover by Wayne McGinnis, Mac'sGraphix
Photos by Michael Murphy

Dedication

I dedicate this book to the glory of Jesus Christ. You are my Lord, Savior, King, Friend and Bridegroom. Jesus you are coming soon and I am eagerly watching for your return and long to be with you. To you be glory, honor and power for ever and ever. Come quickly your bride is waiting.

The following trademarks appear throughout this book: America Online (AOL), CompuServe, Prodigy, Microsoft, Microsoft Network (MSN), MSNBC, WebTV, Microsoft Passport, Sun, Hewlett Packard, HP, Oracle, Sony, Nokia, American Telephone and Telegraph (AT&T), Sprint, MCI, Motorola, Iridium, Cellular One, Cisco, McDonalds, Big Mac, Coke, American Express, VISA, Mastercard, Cirrus Systems, Mini Bank, Mondex, Multos, VisaCash, VeriChip, Applied Digital, Ellipso, Thuraya, Globalstar, ICO, ORBCOMM,. Any exclusion of trademarks referenced in this book was unintentional and it is the intention of the publisher to depose such trademarks herein.

Although the author and publisher have exhaustively researched all sources to ensure the accuracy and completeness of the information contained in this book, we assume no responsibility for errors, inaccuracies, omissions or any other inconsistency herein. Any slights against people or organizations are unintentional.

Attention colleges and universities, religious organizations, and writing and publishing organizations: Quantity discounts are available on bulk purchases of this book for educational training purposes, fund-raising, or gift giving. Special books, booklets, or book excerpts can also be created to fit your specific needs. For information contact Marketing Department, English Channel Press, P.O. Box 461174, Aurora, Colorado 80046-1174, 303-699-3383.

Acknowledgment

Many thanks to my wife Jan, your love and encouragement has been inspirational in helping me complete this book. I am blessed to share my life with you and look forward to growing old together. You are truly a gift from the Lord.

Many thanks to my children, Laura, Allan, Farrah and Austin, you are a blessing to me. I appreciate your patience listening to all of my discoveries and current events. I especially thank my daughter Farrah who envisioned the design for the book cover with my artist Wayne McGinnis.

Many thanks to Linda and Bob for the early editing efforts and comments you shared, I appreciate you both! And special thanks to my pastor Peter Young, my friends at BridgeWay Church, and my professional associates and friends who prayed for me and offered encouragement during this adventure, I greatly value your support.

Table of Contents

Introduction XI

Infrastructure—The Great Differentiator 1

The Financial Industry 25

The Security Industry 75

The Visual Media Industries 115

The Communications Industry 153

Electronic Commerce—The New World Economy 205

Call To Action 225

Appendix 245

About The Author 249

Introduction

When my Lord Jesus first told me that I was to write a book, I was excited but mystified. With a wife, four children, and the recent sale of my business, which left me holding a "very full-time job," I knew that a miracle would be required to pull it off. But, after all, God is still in the business of doing miracles and enabling us to do what He calls us to do. My calling includes sharing with you the mystery of technology relevant to prophecies foretold in Revelation, Chapter 13, pertaining to end-time events. God has made clear to me the interdependencies of various technologies and how they work together to facilitate the infrastructure needed to support these end-time prophecies. He shared with me a picture of a puzzle that will be pieced together as a visual image of His revelation of this mystery. For me, the old saying, "A picture is worth a thousand words," rings true, as this mystery became much clearer with this simple and vivid visual example!

So begins my journey, or should I say the sharing of a 27-year journey that started with my conversion from the Moslem religion and subsequent calling to itinerate evangelism when I was in high school to my current path as a technologist and evangelist. My technology career began in 1979 when I started working in the telecommunications industry. In 1983 I became self employed and for 17 years owned and operated companies that designed, installed, and maintained complex telecommunications and data network solutions for corporations in a variety of vertical markets. During this time, I grew to have a reputation of pursuing cutting-edge technologies. Phrases such as "You have to bleed to lead," "We bleed so you don't have to," "Practice what you preach," "user of the madness," "virtual culture," and "work anytime, anywhere," characterized my business philosophy and endeavors. As the years went on and business and technology evolved, I began to have a notion that if I am in technology and I believe in the written Word of God, I could predict the future of this industry because I possessed the playbook.

I knew that the Bible predicted that there would be a one-world government, or global community, led by the Antichrist and 10 appointed regional kings. I also knew that the world would require an infrastructure that would facilitate an electronic currency and global economy allowing the Antichrist to control the buying and selling of goods throughout the world. Armed with these simple facts, I began to consider what types of things, from a technical perspective, would be required to facilitate these prophecies.

I realized that for these prophecies to be fulfilled, an infrastructure would have to be created that was global in nature, without the limitations of connectivity imposed by our current technological methods. In addition, business applications that will allow the buying and selling of goods and services would need to be created and provided to consumers worldwide. There would also have to be advanced methods of security that would allow people to access the business applications necessary for buying and selling goods and services, anytime, anywhere, without the fear of financial loss.

As I began to reflect on these requirements, I knew that there were a number of holdouts, particularly communication infrastructure, complexity and proliferation of disparate information technology systems and global access to devices that would facilitate cashless buying and security methods. With our fast-paced progression of society, it became evident that our current methods of terrestrial connectivity including copper cabling and fiber-optics would not be sufficient to build this new infrastructure. The cost and the time necessary to deploy these technologies would be a barrier to success. In addition there would need to be a unification, or standardization, of computer operating systems to simplify the development process making it easier to create on-line applications. The purpose of these applications will be to provide customers easier access to products and services on-line. People would also need easier and more available methods of purchasing goods and services without physical currency. Access portals, which I will call any device that allows for the electronic purchase of a product or service, would need to be placed in common areas to service all the functions of life such as the purchase of gasoline, groceries, clothing, and entertainment.

It became clear to me that these various sectors of technology (business applications, communications infrastructure, operating system and networking standards and security) would have to be converged together to create a cohesive, global, electronic business environment that would facilitate instant worldwide communications and e-commerce. The blending, or "convergence," of these technical sectors to create a global community and economy would give rise to the ultimate "killer application." The converged applications will be used by the Antichrist to control and dominate the world persuasively, through deception and great miracles, necessitating the need to bear a mark that will allow the world's inhabitants to buy and sell the very necessities of life—food, shelter, and clothing—electronically (Revelation 13:13-14, 16-17).

This gives new meaning to the word "killer application" because people who embrace this application and choose to accept the mark of the Beast in the end will "BE KILLED" eternally (Revelation 14:9-11). We as technologists have been searching for the "killer application" like archeologists search for the Holy Grail. Little did we know that our relentless pursuit of the "killer application" would have such significance or symbolism relevant to end-time prophecies! Since this revelation, which took place for me in the mid-1980s, I have endeavored to build my career around the convergence of these technologies. I realized that it would simply be a matter of time before the technologists of the world would begin to move in this direction, because it was foretold thousands of years before in the last book of the Bible.

The last 15 years have been exciting for me, as I have watched the fulfillment of this unfold before my very eyes! The advent of the popularity of the Internet, standardization to Internet Protocol (IP) as a globally accepted networking protocol, de facto standards in operating systems, and deployment of wireless technology to facilitate global connectivity and advances in security (your computer identity) techniques are making it all possible!

At no other time in the history of mankind has the world had the technology infrastructure in place to fulfill the prophecies of Revelation, Chapter 13. I believe the signs of the times, the current state of Israel and the Middle East crisis, and the evolution of technology are playing together like a symphony pointing toward the coming of Jesus Christ. Current events in our newspapers, in magazines, and on television read like the fulfillment of the message Jesus delivered to the disciples on the Mount of Olives in Matthew, Chapter 24, (see Appendix). Our world is filled with false prophets and religions, wars, kingdoms rising against kingdoms, famines, and earthquakes in greater quantities than the world has ever experienced in the past. Clearly these signs alone would make you wonder about the nearness of the return of Jesus Christ. But I would have you consider that many of these same events have been going on for centuries and making people wonder for thousands of years if tomorrow will be the day! So what was missing? Why now?

The important element that was missing from the lives of all of those before us, who thought that Jesus would come in their lifetime, was global infrastructure. There has been no other time in history when Satan, working through the Antichrist described in Revelation, has had the technology and infrastructure needed to create a global society available for his use. With such infrastructure he will be empowered to capitalize on world events and mandate that everyone receive a mark (or identification) that would signify worship of him. He will also use this global infrastructure for the control of life's most basic needs, the ability to buy and sell goods electronically (e-commerce). Control of e-commerce, and the creation of electronic currency, will allow the Antichrist to drive home the need to worship him by controlling the world's basic needs for shelter, food, and clothing–in essence, one's very survival.

This is the mystery that God is revealing during our current time in history. I believe that God is calling us to understand and realize the significance of the current state of technology and global infrastructure and with this newfound knowledge to be challenged to look for the return of Jesus Christ through new eyes! Are you looking, or will He surprise you like a thief in the night?

Chapter One

Infrastructure the Great Differentiator

The mystery of the return of Jesus Christ or the apocalyptic end of the Earth, as prophesied in the Bible, has been a subject of curiosity for people around the world for centuries. Countless groups of individuals, who believed they could predict the day when Jesus would come, have put on their white robes, sold their homes, packed up their belongings, and headed for the hills so that they could be ready for the return of Jesus Christ.

People around the world, as they counted down for the arrival of the millennium, thought that on the stroke of midnight, the Y2K bug would bring computer technology worldwide to its knees, creating chaos and mayhem because of the loss of basic services such as electricity, banking, and communications.

Companies upgraded their machinery, computer hardware and software, applications, and programs. Individuals prepared their homes by purchasing generators, heaters, and woodstoves. They stockpiled food and built underground shelters. Billions of dollars were spent worldwide on Y2K readiness initiatives. People all around the world were watching and considering every aspect of this event in attempt to be prepared for the worst.

Some of you may remember the covers of national magazines sensationally depicting individuals with billboards strapped to their chests that said, "The end of the world is near." There was an increase in coverage of religious events discussing the foretelling of prophecy regarding the end of the age. Law-enforcement agencies were preparing for radical and malicious behavior from extremists and religious zealots. The Federal Bureau of Investigation (FBI) even published a paper called Project Megiddo, which outlined in detail things concerning Y2K apocalyptic religious beliefs, apocalyptic cults, and gun control—and offered insights and instruction to law enforcement agencies.

In the end, the clock struck midnight, ushering in a new millennium, and I believe much to the surprise of many, things went relatively smoothly worldwide. Our social structure didn't collapse, there wasn't mayhem and chaos, the banking system didn't collapse, my ATM card still worked, and I wasn't without lights for even a minute–so much for the $2,500.00 generator I purchased that is big enough to power the whole neighborhood! As a matter of fact, I'm reporting this fact secondhand, because when the clock struck midnight, my wife Jan and I were floating on a cruise ship near the Panama Canal enjoying our millennium cruise. I guess it was my way, as a technocrat, of making a political statement regarding my concern about all the Y2K hype.

So what was all that fuss about? Was it just another "end-time" false alarm? It certainly felt that way to many. I submit to you that the Y2K issue was not a false alarm. Rather the entire situation was a needed cleansing or updating of the worldwide technological computing environment as part of building the necessary infrastructure to support end-time prophecies. Up until this time, systems around the world had been installed based on the evolution of the "Information Era." This period in history was characterized by leading computer manufacturers providing their customers with proprietary hardware, operating systems, applications, and networking protocol, making interoperability between competitive computing solutions difficult. As a result, businesses that desired interoperability to conduct business worldwide were encumbered. In essence, they were held hostage to purchase their equipment from their incumbent computer manufacturer. Basically, with their initial investment decision, they "sold their soul to the company store," and the chosen manufacturer loved it!

With the advent of the personal computer (PC) and the growing popularity of the Internet, market pressure began to move manufacturers toward developing and providing open systems solutions. Open systems solutions or open architecture leverage compatible and interchangeable hardware and interpretable software based on industry standards set down by standard bodies such as the Institute of Electrical and Electronic Engineers

(IEEE), International Telecommunications Union (ITU), Telecommunications/Electronic Industry Associations (TIE/EIA), International Standards Organization (ISO), and Bellcore. An example is the PC. Various manufacturers build the PC, but parts from a different manufacturer, in most cases, can be inserted into the system to provide new features or basic operation.

In addition, de facto standards for operating systems emerged based on market penetration—an example would be the popular Microsoft Windows Family, which is operating on most of the PC desktops worldwide. Although an official (independent) standards body did not sanction this software, sheer market pressure dictated that people would develop applications around these operating systems to improve the chance of selling their software products. This is an example of the standards body called "The Golden Rule"—"He who has the gold makes the rules"!

The Internet, which uses Transmission Control Protocol/Internet Protocol (TCP/IP), took off with the Internet craze and forced manufacturers to create their solutions to leverage this protocol (you can think of protocol like a language such as French or English). If their systems used (talked) a different protocol (language), they had to build a gateway, which acts like a translator, allowing their systems to speak TCP/IP, which is the language of the Internet backbone or data highway.

As a result of this response to market pressure, the vast Web of Internet infrastructure can now be leveraged to develop a worldwide backbone or data highway that bridges the gaps between all the various computer protocols which exist around the world on different systems made by different manufacturers. This promotes business relationships and allows for interoperability between computer systems, creating a World Wide Web (WWW) of business applications, which provide goods and services to people throughout the globe.

So why spend time reviewing Y2K and discussing the issues of this particular event? Because Y2K is just one example of a multifaceted plan to develop the infrastructure necessary to support a worldwide e-commerce network. As you will learn in this chapter, the uniqueness of this period in time is all about infrastructure. At no other time in the history of mankind has infrastructure been *so ready* to support a worldwide dictator, such as the Antichrist, as prophesied in the book of Revelation.

Overview of the Technology Chapters

In the next five chapters we will be considering the technical infrastructure necessary to facilitate the control of buying and selling goods and services electronically worldwide. Y2K is just one piece addressing hardware limitations, applications, and database date and time issues. In general, previous limitations of hardware and applications helped encourage adoption and deployment of de facto standards, which may have not been implemented without the fear of loss of revenues because of systems and applications failures. This new, more unified or standardized, operating environment has made the development of business applications used in the global electronic business (e-business) marketplace easier and faster.

Additional technological developments are being made in the financial, communications, security, and visual media sectors of industry. These four areas will be my focal point and fuel the e-commerce initiative, which is at the heart of an electronic global society giving the Antichrist the ability to control the buying and selling of goods and services worldwide. He will leverage this infrastructure by imposing the requirement to have a mark on your forehead or on your right hand. Without the mark, you will not be able to conduct business or purchase the necessities of life. As we proceed, you will see that this mark has great technological significance.

Unraveling the Mystery

Below is a picture of a puzzle that God gave me to illustrate the simplicity of how these major industry sectors are interdependent in facilitating electronic commerce (e- commerce).

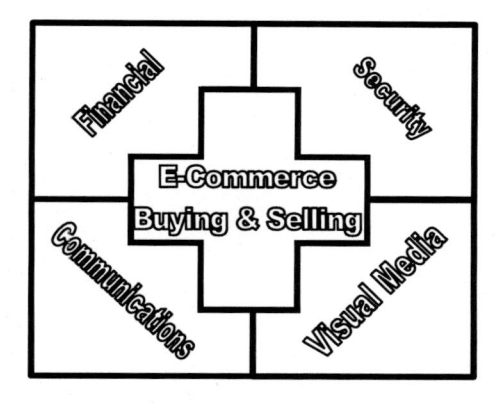

[Diagram: A puzzle showing E-Commerce Buying & Selling at the center, surrounded by four pieces labeled Financial, Security, Communications, and Visual Media.]

Each puzzle piece represents an industry sector. The placement of the pieces, one to another, represent dependencies necessary between each sector to enable e-commerce, which is in the center and intersects all of the respective industries and technologies. Upon completion of the puzzle, a global electronic ecosystem will be created standing ready to fulfill end-time prophecies as outlined in Revelation, Chapter 13.

We will examine in upcoming chapters, one for each puzzle piece, a brief evolution of the industry, the current state of the industry, any technical holdout and its impact on the development of other industries, and the role of the specific industry relevant to the big picture and final solution. We will also consider the interdependencies of the industries, which are motivating the concurrent development of each respective solution in response to market pressure to complete the killer application. Below is an introduction to the upcoming chapters and some thoughts about the uniqueness of infrastructure during this period in history.

The Financial Industry

The conservative and accurate processing of transactions and the electronic transfer of funds worldwide characterize the financial industry. This extremely mature and dependable network eliminates the need for common currency by automatically adjusting for the respective exchange rate. My wife and I traveled to London, put our Automate Teller Machine (ATM) card in the machine, and out like candy came the local currency at the current exchange rate within seconds. **So much for the need of one-world currency. We effectively have that right now through the use of technology. The rest is semantics.**

The financial community will soon rely on the developing security industry because of the necessity of protecting our electronic funds and our digital identity because of the electronic globalization of commerce.

The Security Industry

The security industry, which is in the technical limelight, is being developed to support computer applications and other electronic portals, which are used to access and purchase goods and services electronically. As previously discussed in the Introduction, **I define an access portal as any device that allows for the electronic purchase of a product or service**. This is extremely important, especially with the recent rise in digital identity crimes. It is necessary for this industry to provide users with an irrefutable identification (ID), which can be used **simply** within the electronic marketplace to purchase goods and services without fear of financial loss. Current security models have many limitations, are becoming grossly inadequate, and will eventually evolve toward physical implants, which will allow for irrefutable access to data systems as well as a myriad of other features such as Global Positioning Systems (GPS) tracking and Smart Card functionality.

A Smart Card has a chip capable of containing all types of information such as your Social Security number, driver's license number, medical information (vital signs, allergic reactions, and medical records), credit card information, and business preferences. The chip is read/writeable so the contents can be updated as needed without card replacement in real time at a vendor location, via computer, ATM machine or other compatible download devices. Smart Card technologies are currently being used and developed by MasterCard, Visa, and American Express, as illustrated in recent national marketing campaigns.

The security industry will also serve the Visual Media Industries, as this includes computer and television access to electronic business portals for purchasing goods, services, and entertainment.

The Visual Media Industry

The visual media Industry is a name I have coined for this book and my message, and it represents the convergence of multimedia devices such as a television (TV) or computer and the entertainment industries and/or vendors that will provide goods and services via these visual multimedia portals. We will discuss the imminence of computer technology being converged into the television, which we have comfortably sat in front of like couch potatoes for 50 years.

When you finish reading this section you will have a new understanding of the words "operant conditioning." Before you know it, you'll be ordering pizza, checking your electronic mail (e-mail), talking to Grandma, and transacting banking business through the push of a button on your remote control.

The visual media Industry is extremely dependent on the communications and security Industries. The Communications Industry will solve the last mile problem, (last mile is defined as the final connection into your home, apartment or business from your local communication service provider. The connection can be wireless, cable, satellite, copper, or fiber) providing high-speed bandwidth (a big fat pipe for sending all of our visual stuff) to allow for on-demand programming, interactive TV applications, e-mail, web browsing and shopping, telephone functionality, and video conferencing. This technology will be able to effectively deliver these services anywhere in the world without wires. Look, Mom, no hands!

The Communications Industry

The Communications Industry represents the technology that connects everything together and is the glue that makes worldwide communications possible. The Communications Industry is currently the technological holdout because of the limitations of fiber and copper technologies and their inability to provide broad bandwidth connectivity to every inch of the globe in a timely and cost-effective manner. Recent developments in this marketplace in the area satellite communications and other wireless technologies eliminate the last mile dilemma by providing high-capacity broad bandwidth services to any user anywhere in the world. These networks will facilitate the streaming video broadcast programming (for TV programming), data communications (to provide access to applications to conduct business), and telecommunications (for voice conversations), generally making the world a smaller place.

The race for ownership of the sky is under way right now with the list of players reading like a Who's Who of communications and computing. The players are speculating that the successful deployment of these satellite networks will bring fortune beyond their wildest dreams. I'd like to say the fortunes might even surpass Bill Gates' Microsoft legacy, but he's already invested in many of these major initiatives, so, too bad, guys, he'll probably stay number one on the "richest man in the world list"! You go, Bill!

The communications industry sector is significant (a major dependency for you project managers out there) to the completion and maturity of the global e-commerce marketplace. Most systems are scheduled to be completed in the first decade of the new millennium with a scramble for sooner rather than later. The urgency is caused by market pressure for global high-speed connectivity and fear of financial loss because of lost market share.

This is a high-stakes game in both the natural and the supernatural realms. In the natural, there are fortunes to be made or lost (fueled by greed). For example, the life expectancy on the Low Earth Orbit (LEO) satellites are projected to be 5 to 10 years at a projected cost of $9 billion for just one of the numerous networks being deployed. In the supernatural, the Antichrist will depend on wireless technology to facilitate worldwide communications and to maintain control of e-commerce in the wake of major seismic activity predicted in the Bible.

These earthquakes will occur throughout the 7 short years of the Tribulation and will wreak havoc on wired (copper and fiber) infrastructure, crippling communications and commerce that rely solely on terrestrial infrastructure. So you think this is all happening by chance? Think again! Somebody knows the game plan and believes what the Bible says! Do you?

The E-Commerce Global Marketplace

E-commerce, which is at the heart of the puzzle, is the killer application and will be discussed in detail. Philosophically, this is where all of the technologies converge to form a usable worldwide suite of business applications and services that will create an electronic marketplace. This is the most visually apparent piece of the puzzle because we are being bombarded with it day in and day out through advertisements on the TV, in magazines and newspapers, and on billboards and cereal boxes. Everywhere we look, it's "e-something" or, better yet, it's "e-everything"!

E-commerce will touch every walk of life as we know it today, including restaurants, retailers, service providers, financial institutions, governments, and on and on—it's not just the WWW and web surfing. This elaborate worldwide network will also provide us knowledge on all types of subject matter as prophesied in the Old Testament thousands of years ago. It will become part of the fabric of our new global society, breaking down international barriers from both political and economic standpoints.

We will review how all of these technologies are being concurrently developed on similar timelines to converge together to form the necessary infrastructure to complete this global e-commerce environment in the immediate future. When you stand back and look at it from a distance, it's like a beautifully orchestrated piece of music with a climactic crescendo or a beautifully engineered project plan with every dependency and contingency taken into account. Years of preparation and leveraging of trends such as Moore's Law—which says that performance doubles and the price is cut in half every 18 months have been at work for 30 years to bring this about. The craze of the Internet and the speed at which applications can and are being developed is astounding. Technology on all fronts, many of which we will not discuss in this book, are all arriving on the scene, ready to take their place in history.

This electronic marketplace is not only about commerce but is a bridge between countries and cultures, making the world a smaller place. All around the globe this technical phenomenon, which has been adapted faster than any other technology previously used, has impacted the world. People can send e-mail or instant message (IM) around the globe, use the Internet to place a free telephone call, and use free software to videoconference with a friend and to gain access to a plethora of free information exploring every subject imaginable!

Why are we attracted to it? Why does it offer so much? Why will we sit for hours in front of a screen that's moving so slowly it aggravates us beyond all comprehension? Do you give up? Because it has to be! You need to think it's wonderful, you need to feel that it saves you time and improves your life, you need to think it's a great source for information, and you need to be concerned about financial loss when using the Beast. Why? Because you're being conditioned for what's coming in the future. I don't think it will be hard for you to accept the things I'm going to discuss in this book. I believe you will eventually want them or feel you need them!

Now I know some of you are thinking, "Who is he to tell me what I will want?" Right? You think you are one of those special people who cannot be put into a box or do not like to be told what they are going to do as if they have no control. Well, let me tell you. You will be put in this box, because, in the end, you will only have two choices:

One choice is to receive a mark of the beast signifying your worship of the Antichrist and his new world government. In trade you will be able to continue buying and selling the basic necessities of life (Revelation 13:15-17) and thus condemning yourself to eternal separation from your creator and death (Revelation 14: 9-11).

"He was given power to give breath to the image of the first beast, so that it could speak and cause all who refused to worship the image to be killed. He also forced everyone, small and great, rich and poor, free and slave, to receive a mark on his right hand or on his forehead, so that no one could buy or sell unless he had the mark, which is the name of the beast or the number of his name. This calls for wisdom. If anyone has insight, let him calculate the number of the beast, for it is man's number. His number is 666" (Revelation 13:15).

"A third angel followed them and said in a loud voice: "If anyone worships the beast and his image and receives his mark on the forehead or on the hand, he, too, will drink of the wine of God's fury, which has been poured full strength into the cup of his wrath. He will be tormented with burning sulfur in the presence of the holy angels and of the Lamb. And the smoke of their torment rises forever and ever. There is no rest day or night for those who worship the beast and his image, or for anyone who receives the mark of his name" (Revelation 14:9-11).

The other choice is to refuse the mark and suffer persecution and physical death (Revelation 13:15). Persecution will come to anyone who holds onto any belief system other than that which is being required by the tyrannical dictator who is the Antichrist. The Bible promises that for those who are martyred (beheaded) for their testimony of

Jesus Christ, a special crown or reward will be awaiting them in Heaven (Revelation 20:04). **If you are not a believer in Jesus Christ and you do not think that you are going to take this mark, for whom or what cause will you die?**

I mentioned earlier while discussing the Communications Industry that the stakes are high and the plan is under way. God is in control of the universe, and He has given Satan authority over the Earth as a result of his fall from heaven (where God dwells). Satan is astute about the Scriptures and understands what they mean. And I believe that in spite of himself, he knows that the Scriptures are true and his days are numbered. But Satan, from the dawn of time, has desired to be worshiped as God and is determined to have his day in the sun, even if only for just a few short years.

Satan is influencing the world and is watching the signs of the times, as we are encouraged to do in the Scriptures as presented in Matthew, Chapter 24. He, like, mankind, is unknowing of the day or hour that Jesus Christ will triumphantly return to Earth, but he is closely watching the signs, just as we are encouraged to do in the Bible.

Satan also understands the Scriptures and knows what is foretold regarding the mark of the beast and seismic activity that will used to judge the Earth during the tribulation; he is planning accordingly. As an analyst, I could go on for a long time drawing analogies about this subject, but I want you to begin your thought processes regarding the things that are happening in the world around you. My hope is that you will come to the same conclusion that I have—that things are not happening by chance, but rather by design.

The industries described in the following chapters and their harmonious interweaving or convergence to form a worldwide electronic infrastructure will give the Antichrist the ability to control commerce and to have a communications platform from which to deliver his message to the inhabitants of the Earth. Because of the hardships and judgments that will be taking place during the Tribulation, many will begin to look at the antichrist, because of his actions, as a savior or deity. At the midpoint of the 7-year judgment, he will enter Solomon's temple, which will be rebuilt on Jerusalem's temple mount, and will declare himself God, requiring all to worship him and to take his mark.

I want you to be prepared for this event, so that when it takes place, you will have a point of reference from which to look in the midst of the chaos and crisis. The Bible is clear that many will be deceived during this time because of the antichrist's charisma, supernatural miracles, and resurrection from assassination (Revelation, Chapter 13).

My stewardship with this message is the revelation of the current state of technology as one piece of infrastructure that is now being developed to facilitate the imminent coming of Jesus Christ and the tribulation or judgment period that will last just 7 short years.

The title of this chapter is "Infrastructure, the Great Differentiator." Because infrastructure is the great differentiator, careful consideration should be given to the imminence of the return of Jesus Christ. I have mentioned before that there is no other time in history in which so many pieces of the puzzle are in place to give the Antichrist the infrastructure needed to be a world dictator.

It is not simply the technology sectors, but rather the sum total of numerous parts taking place on a variety of fronts that seem to make this time in history unique. I know you are saying, "I've heard this message for years, and the church has been watching for Jesus Christ for 2000 years—so why now?" What is so special about now?

If you are asking this question, it is a good one, and I will try to give you an answer. I believe that the intrigue and mysticism of the book of Revelation has kept her readers and theologians interested for years—and by design! I believe, as we look back over history, that there were cultures and kingdoms that believed that they were the center of the universe–such as Rome and Egypt, for example. Many of these kingdoms built infrastructure (within their technological and physical limitations) and conducted military campaigns to dominate "their world." Society was evil and there were earthquakes and other signs aligning with Matthew, Chapter 24 but Jesus has yet to return. So what is different now?

Until this century, many of the technologies needed to produce a global community simply did not exist. The 20th century gave rise to motorized locomotion. Steamships, trains, and the automobile provided mankind with the first major change in transportation in 6,000 years. Yet that wasn't enough to provide a global community. The advent of the airplane in the early 1900s and space travel in the 1960s revolutionized man's ability to circumnavigate the globe. Now a traveler can fly anywhere in the world within 36 hours (including layovers), and supersonic planes make transatlantic trips (New York to London) in 4 hours. With such inventions, the world seems like a smaller place.

Technology, which we will discuss at length in this book, is creating a communications fabric that provides instantaneous communications and business transactions bridging time and space, political boundaries, and economics, affording us a real-time look at our world. A great example is the instant Cable News Network (CNN) live news reports, which take you into the muck and mire of world events in the comfort of your living room! Recent coverage of the invasion of Iraq by the allied forces was unprecedented in history. Embedded reporters on the front lines provided the world blow-by-blow coverage as it happened.

Anyone with the TV today can feel a part of a global community.

The political climate and governing bodies like the United Nations are proponents for a one-world global community. The arguments for humanity, world peace, disarmament, and elimination of poverty are all being discussed as part of major initiatives. A visit to the United Nations web site and an awareness of listening to the words of our politicians makes this premise of a global community not far fetched. The only thing missing is a worldwide crisis that would motivate countries to throw down their sovereignty and consider the better good of humanity! Because I dislike politics, I will not belabor this point, but rest assured that the notion of the one-world government has been considered and is awaiting an event and a charismatic leader to capitalize on such a thought. Can we guess who that might be?

Yes, of course, the lists of standard indicators are also running rampant! With wars and rumors of wars, and kingdoms rising against kingdoms, never in history have there been more military conflicts around the world, including the most recent invasion of Iraq making the Middle East an even greater hot bed for conflict. Famine and starvation are on the rise. Plagues—including Acquired Immune Deficiency Syndrome (AIDS), a leading killer of young and middle aged adults worldwide—are being under projected for their impact on humanity. New strains of drug-resistant, infectious diseases such as tuberculosis are emerging on the medical scene. The most recent outbreak of Severe Acute Respiratory Syndrome (SARS) in China, North America and Europe is just a sign of things to come.

New forms of cancer, particularly skin cancer like melanoma, are on the rise. Earthquakes have occurred in greater frequency and intensity in this century than at any other time in history. This is a critical indicator, as the tectonic plates around the world are positioning themselves (pressure is building) for the catastrophic events that will take place during the tribulation.

The rise of violence worldwide and the desensitization of our children and adults as a result of our graphically violent visual media industries is another indicator. Before the flood, which was God's last global judgment, the times were said to be violent. You just need to look at what is playing in the theaters, on TV, and in the video arcades (or games being played on your TV at home). I'm confident that you will not go very long without seeing or hearing about someone being blown away, murdered, or beaten up.

The heightened conflict between Israel and Palestine is also an indicator. Israel has partially returned to the land (1948) in fulfillment of biblical prophecies. The main points of contention are the control and occupation of the holy city. This is an age-old battle with no end in sight between two cultures that are generally not very compromising. You can expect this conflict to continue to grow until a charismatic, well-spoken leader facilitates peace and signs a 7-year peace treaty with Israel, guaranteeing her safety. Can you guess who this might be?

So is this time in history unique? I think that when you combine the normal signs—which seem to have existed throughout history—and the recent developments of this century—particularly transportation, technology, and a spirit of global community, it's very feasible to believe that Jesus Christ could come in our lifetime, even tonight! I'm looking expectantly and believe that we are in an exciting and unique period in the history of mankind.

My hope is that after you read this book, you will never look at current events; your checkbook; an ATM machine; a swipe reader at the restaurant, grocery story, or gas pump; the Internet; your TV and remote control; your computer; or your user name and password the same way again.

I either want them to be a warm reminder of the imminent coming of your Savior, Jesus Christ, and a challenge to serve him faithfully, or a haunting image of God's impending judgment on the Earth and its inhabitants who do not have a personal relationship with Jesus Christ.

Do you think that sounds hard and pretentious? It might be, if I did not believe that every foretold prophecy in the Bible is true. But I do believe that they are true, and as a result, I believe that this message is timely and merciful, yet again showing God's endless outreach for our souls and the relevance of the Bible for today. God wants us to be ready for the return of His Son, Jesus Christ, to this earth. He is long suffering and would not have any man perish. Rather, He desires that all have eternal life through His Son. I encourage you to read on, because when you finish this book, you will understand that everything around you is part of an intricate, detailed plan orchestrated by God Himself and His enemy, the devil. The question is, "Are you ready?" Or will Jesus return and surprise you like a thief in the night?

Chapter Two

The Financial Industry

The Evolution of the Financial Industry

In this chapter, I will review the evolution of banking relevant to methods and adaptation of handling hard currency to that of electronic processing of business transactions (or electronic currency) used when purchasing goods and services. The purpose of this evolutionary history is to give you a sense of how the implementation of technology has created a paradigm change in banking in which customers have moved from the use of paper currency to electronic funds transfer. It will also give you a sense of our global community, as you will see that customers have universal access to their funds in any country with a similar technology.

As I began to research the history of banking for this chapter, one thing became clear—banking has a well-documented and rich heritage in our world. This is not surprising, as we often have great concern for monetary issues in our lives. There are many old sayings about money, such as: "It takes money to make money," "Money makes the world go around," "There isn't any problem that can't be solved with money," and "Money can't buy you love." And I am sure there are many more. I am not going to dare to delve into the complexities of this industry, discussing the nuts and bolts of what goes on in the back room. Rather, I am going to focus on the transformational changes that came to banking as a result of technology used in this century. My objective is to expose you to the subtle migration toward, and the acceptance and utilization of, the electronic or cashless model versus that which has been done with consumables or common currency during the past 4,000 years.

Early Banking History

Webster's dictionary first notes the word "bank" appearing at about the 13th century. Credible instances of banking appear as early as 3000 B.C. and 2000 B.C. in temples in Mesopotamia, where the materials used to store and borrow were common day commodities.

Banking may be one of the oldest professions in the world, and, at its essence, considers the basic attributes of humanity: trusting in borrowing. Banking in the simplest sense involves the lending of someone's excess currency to a trusted individual who will pay interest, in whatever form that may be, for the temporary use of these excess funds. In the earliest days in man's history, before the development of common currency, payment was made in the form of other valuables such as grain, usable consumables or services. This concept of lending and repayment seems to be at the core of humanity, and most of us can likely reflect back and see our local childhood loan shark loaning extra change for a return on the investment of dime-store candy.

The Role of the Financial Industry in Global Electronic Commerce

The financial industry will play an extremely important role in the development and use of a global e-commerce infrastructure. The financial community includes traditional banking institutions and pseudo-financial institutions such as investment bankers, mortgage bankers, and private investment communities. In general, anyone who provides financial services in which they charge a fee for service, charges interest for lending money, provides credit, offers savings accounts (which can be arbitraged for gain by the financial institution), or provides transaction services to merchants for credit and debit card transactions will be considered in this book as a part of the financial industry.

The banking industry, in the traditional sense, which offers its customers savings and checking accounts, credit card services, and ATM and debit card services will be the main focal point for most of the discussions of this chapter. This is not designed to minimize the importance of the other financial organizations and investment communities, but traditional banking is the most visual and regularly used by the populace on a day-to-day basis to support the basic necessities of life.

The banking industry has grown to be trusted by its patrons and is characterized by conservative and reliable methods for processing financial transactions across the street or around the world. The banking industry will continue to function in a large number of areas pertinent to e-commerce and will be a major contributor to the success of e-commerce as it manages people's most important asset—their capital! Banking provides many services today that will facilitate e-commerce and provide electronic currency globally. Some examples include:

- Global technological infrastructure
- Global currency exchange-rate services
- Merchant services and access portals for purchasing goods and services
- Direct deposits from employers
- Credit card services
- ATM and debit card services
- Smart Card services
- On-line banking services
- Security methods and practices.

I will be discussing these items in more detail in the upcoming sections of this chapter.

The banking industry will continue to influence the migration of our society from paper currency to electronic currency. This is in direct response to global market pressure for a convenient and secured e-commerce environment. The motivation to change will come in the form of low interest offers and improved exchange rates, which will aid in the acceptance and adaptation of this new model. Because our society is so credit burdened, these low interest rates will bring some much-needed, cash flow relief with acceptance of the new program offers.

In Europe, the recent move to the Euro, which is the unification of currency in the region, was first available as electronic currency prior to the release of physical currency. The financial industries in the area made the new currency available electronically via Smart Card technology, leveraging a new "standards compliant" electronic purse (Common Electronic Purse Specifications [CEPS] will be discussed later in this chapter). The institutions will use offers of improved exchange rates, which is like giving their customers money, for using the new electronic method of exchanging payment. This currency unification was impetuous for the development of Smart Card or chip technology in Europe.

As customers use the newly offered technology, by means of helpful motivation, it will change their paradigm drawing them closer to a total electronic or cashless mentality because of the ease, convenience and security of these new services and programs.

These new programs—marketed under the flag of value-added services, or differentiating features of the institution—will increase transaction revenue and increase profitability for the institution. As a result, bankers will continue to create new services for their customers and merchants, leveraging technology to create a source of reoccurring revenue on a per-transaction basis for the institution.

Transaction revenue will become of great importance as more and more merchants install *"access portals"* (such as a swipe reader or scanning device) to conduct business and process electronic transactions. Banks will be able to develop charging models for both customers and merchants, giving an incentive for paper currency to become less and less prevalent. This is extremely important and is a major motivator for the banking industry, as competition has become very competitive worldwide in recent decades.

Financial institutions will develop "loyalty programs" for merchant members. These programs will leverage chip technology or Smart Card capabilities to offer real-time incentives to customers as they purchase goods and services. With this type of feature, a customer can make a purchase and receive free merchandise or discounts immediately when paying for such services, based on their past history of shopping at the specific merchant's establishment.

Emerging chip technology will promote one card to do it all—credit, debit, electronic purse, loyalty programs, personal identification for access and computer login, personal profiles, and medical history. Just think. With so much in one card, you may never want to leave home without it. And for everything else, there is MasterCard.[i]

We will discuss, in upcoming sections of this chapter, banking's dependencies on other industry sectors, particularly communications and security. The concurrent development of these industries will harmoniously provide an electronic solution that is flexible, virtual, and secure.

Keep in mind that because this new economy ultimately will depend on electronic currency (some have suggested even a unified currency), it will depend on the existing good reputation and success of the banking community. In reality, we have a global currency now in practice because I can use my credit card or debit card anywhere in the world to purchase goods and services at the then-current, daily exchange rate. This service is automatically provided by my bank and technologically serves as a bridge to currency disparities.

Friends, an electronic marketplace without cash is not far fetched. As a matter of fact, the banking community has been training you for this event for quite a number of years and stands ready to serve you! Worldwide market pressure for global expansion has created communications and security solutions that will soon eliminate all the barriers. It won't be long before you never hear the jingle of change in your pocket again. At this point, the exclusive use of electronic currency is more an issue of customer perception and a paradigm change rather than a technological limitation. Soon the banks will motivate you financially to change your banking habits, encouraging conformity into the new electronic era. Just watch for your new Smart Card offer in the mail and that low 0% interest rate. How can you help but love your banker? He is always doing such nice things for you! What I really miss are the free toasters.

The Current State of the Banking Industry

The banking industry is the most mature technology sector for the enabling of an electronic cashless society via the use of electronic currency. The industry has been evolving slowly and steadily over many years, changing the paradigm in which we make purchases and conduct business for life's necessities. This subtle evolution of banking is important to notice as it represents a gradual adaptation from the exchange of material currency (cash), which a person possesses in his or her wallet or pocket, to that of electronic currency, which a person may never physically touch, because of the direct deposits into their bank accounts and electronic payment methods.

These new electronic payment methods are still characterized as cash or credit because you have the choice of having payments automatically deducted from your bank checking account or using your debit card, which is, in effect, "your cash account." Or you can choose to use credit, which is not your cash, but a line of credit available to you for which you pay interest. At the end of the month, you have a choice. You can pay the credit card bill in full, thus saving interest charges, or let the bank automatically bill you for the appropriate interest charges. Payment for credit services are taken from your cash account and paid via check, money order, or electronic payment methods.

Do you notice the similarities of practice in naming and payments? Your money is still referred to as cash, and other people's money is still referred to as credit, yet, in many cases, your cash moves from your employer to your bank to the vendor of goods and services without ever passing through your hands. Now rather than digging out that wad of bills or jingling change from your pocket, you simply pull out your "handy dandy" plastic card (alias credit, ATM, debit, or Smart Card) and put it into the gas pump, the grocery store checkout stand, your local McDonalds, or a vending machine and just like that, you are zooming to your next location with a full tank of gas, tonight's dinner in the trunk, and a hot Big Mac, fries, and a Coke by your side. "It doesn't get much better than that!"

For sake of walking down memory lane, let's look briefly at the steps of evolution that we have adapted to in the name of convenience, security, social compliance, market pressure, and the like.

Cash and Local Banking

This is where we started, and for thousands of years, we have conducted business in this manner. We have been paid for our work efforts by our employers, who would go to the bank (or their favorite place to hide money) and pull out what they owe us for the day, week, or month. This payment would be exchanged for our labor services. After receiving our cash payment in physical currency, we would then commence to deposit this in a bank, for safe keeping of course, because we would not want someone to rob us and "take our money." In return, the bank would pay us interest on certain types of accounts and would use our money, which was sitting in a long-term savings account, to loan to others in the form of credit for their purchases. The bank, to create revenue for this service, would charge the borrower more than they paid their savings account customers for putting money into the bank, and so goes the industry to this day. Don't forget, that because we were still dealing in cash and did not have the convenience of the ATM machine, you would retain some cash for daily use (and carry this in a safe place)—not too much, because you would hate to be robbed, after all, you don't have the option of "American Express Travelers Cheques," which can be replaced if "lost or stolen" because they have not been invented yet. Your only banking option, at this time in history, is to go back to your local bank and deduct additional physical currency from your bank accounts. The teller would hand you "cold, hard cash" to use as needed or until it runs out, whichever comes first. Because time hasn't changed much over the years, it is likely the latter.

Checks and Local Banking

Somewhere along the way, for the security, convenience, and benefit of knowing how much you spent along life's way, the checking account was born. This was an interesting phenomenon, in that it was not much different than what we were accustomed to, but now, rather than carrying around physical currency to make purchases, we would carry around a little book of papers in a plastic folder along with the toaster the bank gave us for opening our checking account. Vendors were encouraged by market pressure from consumers—because of our desire to use and enjoy this newly discovered convenience—to accept checks so that they could retain the customers' loyalty. Do you remember hearing "Do you take checks?" or seeing the sign that said "NO CHECKS?"

A consumer would need to verify whether a vendor took checks or not, because with every new method, there are always holdouts for cash. Merchants were leery about taking checks, because sometimes the signature on the check (which promised the merchant that there was money in the bank) was a lie, and the check would "bounce." This term means that the person writing the check had insufficient funds in the account to pay the merchant for the goods and services received. The merchant now had to recover the loss from the person or take a loss for nonpayment. This led to a chain reaction of events, and the banking industry rose to meet the problem of controlling the issuance of bad checks, while helping merchants feel comfortable about taking checks.

Check-handling fees and laws began to emerge. Banks and merchants would charge their customers a fee for having to handle a bounced check. Today this fee is approximately $25.00 to the merchant and $25.00 to the bank. This could become a large sum of money quickly, depending on your stroke of luck. Generally, if you bounce a check, a few checks bounce, not just one, so before you know it, you could have $100.00 or more in bounced check fees. Now this was always intriguing for me to think about because it seemed so silly. You write a check for something, and for whatever reason—and there are many, most of which are caused by carelessness—the checks bounce. Now you are faced with the bank and merchants charging you more money, apparently money that you did not have in the first place, for their goods and services.

To keep this little process working, bad check laws (developed by merchants prosecuting nonpaying customers for fraud) and check guarantee cards (issued by banks to customers) gave merchants the tools they needed to protect themselves against losses from bad checks. This was important because now the banks are realizing that this has become a revenue stream. Customers who bring their cash to the bank and deposit this cash into their checking accounts are now paying service charges for the convenience and safety of writing checks, not to mention fees for bouncing checks. And because things tend to revolve in circles, the merchants' pressure on banks to secure their payments for bad checks gave rise to a check guarantee card, which was required by most places that accept checks. Maybe you remember hearing "Do you take checks?" "Yes, with a check guarantee card." This card, when used automatically because of insufficient funds in the account, would charge interest to the customer for the privilege of protecting their good name and eliminating the bouncing of a check and all of the associated outrageous fees. Isn't life wonderful?

At this stage, people are getting accustomed to using alternate payment methods for purchases. It is still perceived as cash because it requires that you have the funds in your back account, but you are using an alternative method of exchanging currency with the vendors. Vendors are also being trained and conditioned not to take cash, which means that banks can continue the evolution process, which will eventually charge merchants a fee for taking alternative methods of payment (e.g., credit card merchant fees). In a sense, the banks get us coming and going. I guess that is where they came up with phrases such as *"It takes money to make money."*

Consumers, at this point in banking history, are now getting comfortable with the process. You feel secure about carrying around less cash, your toaster is still working, and, as a matter of fact, you changed your banking location, opened a special savings account, and are now enjoying a new microwave oven. Banks have shown you that they can maintain almost perfect ledger accounts for checking and savings balances. I personally have had almost perfect history with my banks. Almost every mistake has always been mine and not the bank's. I applaud the banking industry for such accuracy.

Banking customers are now getting excited about the use of their check register, which should show them where all of their money is going each month. This is helpful for budgeting, tax record keeping, and 1,000 other household uses. Now, instead of getting to the end of the week and wondering where all your cash has gone, you have a convenient place to look at all of your spending activity. With so much benefit, who needs cash?

Reflection: I hope you can clearly see the evolution and dependency in this section. It was a first step to positioning the age of plastic, which we will discuss soon. Think about what has taken place here! Society had a simple method of receiving and exchanging currency for thousands of years. This method was simple and clear—you got paid, and you spent your money until it was gone. You earned more money the next week, and the process started all over again.

But we have exchanged this method for being charged a fee to deposit our money into an institution that, on our behalf, makes payments to vendors, charges us if we make a mistake or are careless and overdraw our account (rightfully so), extends us credit, and charges a fee for using money that is not ours. This conditions us to live beyond our means. Are you getting the picture? There is nothing simpler about these newer concepts, yet we are blinded or required by the forward motion of society to conform to such ideas. Yes, American Express Travelers Checques and the ability to put a "stop payment" on a check is a great feature for minimizing the risk of loss, but at what cost? People have been carrying their money, hiding it in mattresses, and digging holes in their back yard to bury it for years. Maybe that wasn't all bad, but as you will see, it would not give rise to the type of infrastructure or processes needed to create a cashless society that will be used during the last days to control your ability to buy and sell consumables for life's basic requirements. We have been conditioned to accept these methods for our convenience and will continue to be trained to accept more and more electronic methods of payments because of fear of loss and unification of global markets.

Credit and Global Banking

Credit—or what I call the "age of plastic"—has been placed here for functional discussion, as this is not logistically where it started. The concepts of credit are almost as old as the origins of life. Someone with excess goods or money lent to someone with needs in exchange for payment in the form of currency, traded services and interest. Interest, in its simplest form, is the cost of money. Someone with money (or in earlier times, with consumables, shelter, or land puts a value on the loan, and you agree to pay this back over a period of time. It introduces concepts like collateral, which was designed to give the lender some protection if you broke your promise. You put up something as collateral with value in exchange for the loan. If you did not make your payments, the lender had legal rights to take ownership of the collateral.

The premise of collateral, or security, was fear of loss. It was thought that if you had something to lose (such as your house, car, or furniture), you would either pay your bill or think twice about borrowing money in the first place. Conversely, today there has been a major divestiture from this principal with the advent of the credit card, which in most cases is an unsecured loan. The lack of security—or the collateral required to obtain this credit line—has created irresponsible spending and a sea of credit card debt that has a chokehold on society's finances. With nothing to lose, you simply spend until you are at the brink of financial ruin. Then you declare bankruptcy, the creditors (banks and credit card companies) write down (or take losses) on the debt you owe, and over time you re-establish credit and begin the process all over again, or hopefully learn your lesson.

For such risk (based on actuaries) and the freedom of unsecured loans, the banks and credit card companies charge interest rates for these cards that make it almost impossible for someone on a fixed salary to ever get out from under the burden of *"maxed out"* credit cards at 15%-18% interest. This is the banks' strategy with credit cards. If you are a good credit risk, which means you pay your bills on time, they shower you with a large credit line with the hope that you will max yourself to the limit of your cash flow, making only minimum payments for years or forever. Think about this, and ask yourself if you are in this trap or if you feel like you are drowning in debt–it is bondage to this world's system.

This strategy will be very important and will be discussed in upcoming sections of this chapter when you see how the banks will move you to different methods of electronic payments, particularly "Smart Cards" by making low or "0%" interest rate offers to accept their card. A reduction from 18% interest to 0% or near 0% will greatly improve your cash flow, provide great motivation to change, and make your bank seem like a hero. I hope you are beginning to see the subtle, intricate plan or evolution that is taking place here.

So, in reality, the discussion of credit could have been placed in the beginning of the evolution cycle, but I think it flows well here because in modern times credit has risen to new significance and has been pivotal in moving us toward e-commerce or a cashless society.

Credit has always been in our lives in one form or another. A common example was the local general store that provides a credit account to local consumers, which probably started because of the seasonal nature of payments made to farmers and ranchers. The merchant would run an account, and when the crops came in or the cattle were sold, the customer would pay down his debt. Nothing changes. The merchant still had the risk of bad debts. Crops may have been destroyed, sales prices may have been lower than expected, and cattle may have died. The merchant would then decide how much credit could be extended to limit his risk, and the customer would offer an interest payment in the form of cash, cattle, or crops. This relationship centered on trust and typically addressed life's basic needs of food, shelter, clothes, tools, and materials needed by the customer to perform his trade.

The plastic age—our current place in history—is very different. This has evolved like a roaring lion devouring its prey and leaving a wake of destruction behind it. The plastic age exploits our insatiable drive for immediate gratification thus fueling this crisis. We have been given the means though modern-day, unsecured credit to have "what we want when we want it" so that we can enjoy it right now, even if we do not have the money to pay for the purchase! We simply need to be able to make minimum payments, which hold us in bondage almost forever, drowning us in a sea of debt.

The concept of the credit card has been proliferated throughout the free world through an intricate network of banks, merchants, and customers who use this banking infrastructure to purchase goods and services all over the world. We have full technical adaptation, which means that the credit card is globally accepted, heavily used, extremely reliable, very convenient, provides a high level of comfort in transaction accuracy, and is constantly being improved to address market issues such as security and market personalization. We will discuss more on this subject in the section on Smart Cards and the chapters on security and e-commerce.

Basically, credit cards are a way of life, used from the gas pump to the gift shop and everywhere in between. It is global levering, a vast infrastructure of banking networks letting you use the card universally where accepted at the "then-current rate of exchange" in the country you are visiting. Anyone traveling the world knows that it is better, less hassle, and more cost effective to use your credit card rather than trying to exchange foreign currency in a shop that wants to give you a lower-than-fair exchange rate.

In effect, this global network has provided consumers with the ability to purchase goods and services globally without consideration of currency exchange. This ability to globally purchase consumables electronically was a major milestone in a large plan to create the infrastructure needed to fulfill end-time prophecies.

Over the years, after God called me to be an evangelist of the gospel, I have always had interest in end-time prophecy and a specific fascination with the mark of the beast—666—and the associated events that would lead up to this prophecy. One point that I always heard from modern evangelists such as Jack Van Impe and Tim Lehay was to watch for the evolution of a one-world currency. As a young man and until recent years, I watched the news for things such as the development of the Euro currency, which consolidated the currency of a number of European neighbors into one standard currency. This movement certainly was a fulfillment of a prophetic step, showing yet more unification of global markets and the move to a unified currency. In addition to this type of real-world current event, I would like to pose another position for your consideration. I believe that if you are watching for the emergence of a one-world currency, look no longer, because it is here.

As a solution architect in the technology field, which has been my day job since 1979, I focus on the desired business objectives, then leverage people, processes, and technology to obtain these objectives for my clients. When working with a client, my job is to think "out of the box," leveraging the best of a company and using change management to get them to the next step, designing solutions around the business's culture and its customers' perceptions. One challenge I would give to companies retaining my services is: "Don't tell me how to do what you want; tell me what you want or need to achieve, and let me offer you solution alternatives."

So why am I talking about my day job? Well, this book is about technology and the end times. It is discussing current-day happenings and overlaying them on the business objective of Revelation, Chapter 13, which is to leverage an infrastructure that would be used to control the buying of goods and services worldwide.

One element or piece of the puzzle necessary to do this is financial. I believe that functionally and practically, the current financial system solves the problem of one-world currency. The business issue of Revelation, Chapter 13, first considers that there is a global economy, because it is worldwide in touching all walks of life. We currently have a global economy and the ability to purchase goods and services anywhere in the world. This financial model would also require that no matter where you are in the world, you can purchase goods and services and that the infrastructure would have the ability to pay for such services. This also exists today, and technology takes care of the translation, or exchange rate of currency, without getting into the political and sovereignty battles that countries around the world would have if you said we all needed to use the same physical currency. And, finally, you would need the ability to globally turn off someone's ability to purchase goods and services instantly for noncompliance–this exists today and has been working for years! Have you ever had a credit card charge declined because of no available credit or an ATM machine deny use of your card? Well, if this has not happened to you, let me assure you that it can and that it happens frequently. The network exists with the needed intelligence to turn off your very credit existence. This same technology will be leveraged in the last days to control your ability to buy and sell if you do not take the mark of the beast as prophesied in Revelation, Chapter 13.

The credit card was the first step to a global e-commerce network that has worldwide acceptance by merchants and is used by consumers. It was the catalyst for change from physical to electronic currency. It had intelligence, knowing who you are and what you can spend. The bearer of the card should keep this in mind because security issues will soon drive new and improved methods of payments to help eliminate credit card fraud and worse, digital identity crimes.

The credit card also gave rise to three other plastic cards, which moved us yet further toward a cashless or electronic currency model—the ATM, debit card, and Smart Card. In the next section, I will discuss the ATM and debit card. They practically do the same thing, which is to electronically remove funds from your personal bank account to make purchases. We will look at the Smart Card later in this chapter, as it represents the first major paradigm change in the plastic era.

Electronic Currency and Global Commerce

The popularity and success of the credit card and the comprehensive infrastructure in place to support its capabilities could now be leveraged to begin our march toward electronic currency. The evolution from cash to check was step one. The second step was the check guarantee card that was a hybrid, letting you blend your cash with bank credit to further entrench the acceptance and use of this new alternative method of currency by both consumers and vendors. The next step was the ATM card, which focused us on moving away from the need to physically go to the bank to obtain paper currency. Now armed with this new plastic tool, you could walk up to a little machine anywhere and insert the card, enter your secret pin number (secret only if you told no one and the number was not captured through other means) and BadaBoom, BadaBing, out comes the cash, and oh, what convenience! The ATM card made it possible to bank when and where you wanted—no more waiting in lines, no more rushing across town to the bank (after all, they were on banking hours and you were not). In general, it added margin to your busy life. Now isn't that special.

Now this step of evolution is near and dear to my heart because I was closely involved with some of the key players in the early days of this dream's development. In the middle 1980s while operating my first business along with my partner Douglas Cahhal, we provided telephone equipment to a local company in Denver called Minibank. Minibank was a company that was locally beginning to provide ATM services in the Denver community. Now this name may not sound familiar to you unless you lived in the Rocky Mountain region of the United States (U.S.), but the next name might. Minibank was becoming associated with a group called Cirrus Systems. Cirrus Systems was the national (and soon to be international) version of Minibank, representing a network of ATM machines that allowed banks to share their machines to provide customers service all around the globe.

I remember this dream well, as I was blessed with the opportunity to provide these nice folks with a telephone system for their business in the Chicago area, based on a referral from Paul at Minibank.

The name Judy Malone still often comes to mind along with Bruce the founder, Henry, Eric, John and the rest of the gang, whenever I use my ATM card. I feel as if, in a strange kind of way, I had a small part in making this happen. If only those phones could talk.

I remember the discussions of the change in paradigm for the banks. The ATM machines were expensive and were at first a cost to the bank. The bank merely saw this as a necessary evil to be competitive, so a challenge for Cirrus was to create the value proposition for customers and banks to use such technology. I remember some of the marketing promotions—one with Chris Evert Lloyd, the tennis champion, promoting the use of the Cirrus network.

Soon the practicality of this concept began to take off. I remember in my early days of using my ATM card that I would call ahead to see if some of the local banks were members of the Cirrus system. First Interstate Bank was my first experience with this, as they had acquired one of the local banks in my area and had locations in New Mexico, where I was working during travel to this area. I used my card successfully, thanks to the Cirrus relationship, making it possible for me to access my checking account (or my cash) across state lines. The rest is history.

The growing popularity and success of networking ATM machines together provided a convenience to customers that no single banking entity could ever fulfill. It also, over time and with success of use, became a moneymaker for the banks. Now, instead of the machine causing cost to the institution, the machine became a revenue source by allowing the institution to reach more and more areas without the expense of building a staffed branch bank. Simple ATM locations were created, initially bank specific, as there were legal branch banking laws that created restrictions on how customers could deposit money into their accounts. These locations were inexpensive to build, did not require full-time staff, were open 24 hours a day, and provided customers with the features they needed to stay loyal. Revenue profile for the banks changed because of the nature of the beast. Customers of a specific bank were generally not charged a fee for using the ATM machine, because it was an extension of their checking account that made access to their cash with plastic easy and inexpensive. Rather a new alternative source of revenue to the bank was another bank's customer using their machine for cash withdrawals when a customer could not find a machine owned specifically by their personal bank–hence the value of Cirrus System. If the ATM machine displayed the Cirrus logo, a customer could use the machine and be charged an ATM transaction fee on their checking account statement.

The success of Cirrus was later exemplified by their acquisition by MasterCard. You got it, a credit card company now owns an ATM network including banking relationships, infrastructure, and contractual relationships. Beyond this point, I lost track of my friends from Cirrus. I remember that Judy planned to travel back and forth from Chicago to New York, the new home of Cirrus, to finish out her tenure with the company and retire. I never spoke to Bruce personally regarding his success, but having been an entrepreneur myself for years, I imagine that it would always represent a highlight in his career. It is a great joy to see your dream come true and to go global with a concept. My wife has always taught me not to despise small beginnings.

The further evolution of ATM concepts continues to advance, and as you will see later when we discuss debit cards that leverage the global success and acceptance of credit cards by merchants, it takes electronic currency to the next level offering greater impact on our daily lives. The purpose of the ATM card, in the grand scheme of things, was to get you comfortable with electronic banking methods including deposits and withdrawals of your cash from machines rather than from people. The network has proved to be accurate and convenient since its inception in the early 1970s, giving rise to a desire for yet greater convenience and function. To meet customer demands for greater access, machines are now everywhere, including grocery stores, hotels, gas stations, airports, and movie theaters—basically, anywhere you might be where access to your cash could facilitate a purchase from the specific merchant.

Today you are never too far from your cash even if you are out of the country. This method, however, still dictates that you access the machine, get physical currency, and make your purchase from the merchant in cash. You are, however, a little closer to not hearing the jingle of change in your pocket, and the wad of cash in your wallet may be smaller because why should you carry around so much cash when it is so easy to get?

So with so much convenience, who needs more? Well, a society of excess, of course. Why waste your time going to a machine to take out cash when you could just put your plastic card into a swipe reader, or what I call an access portal, and make your purchase. This would save you a step in your busy day, negating the need to visit the ever-present ATM machine, which is in almost every location you could imagine.

The premise of electronic currency and the elimination of cash is not far fetched. As a matter of fact, we are being moved to this slowly by providing more and more universal access portals for purchase. I remember saying to myself, back when I became associated with Cirrus Systems, that all we need now is swipe readers in the grocery stores, at the gas pumps, and in restaurants; then who needs cash? Well, just look around, and you will see what I mean. A recent billboard by the McDonalds restaurant franchise shows a math formula of three pictures being added together: the golden arches logo + a "Big Mac" + the

MasterCard logo = their tag line—"A smile is just a swipe away." I have been waiting for that promotion a long time—"A smile is only a swipe away." It doesn't get any more real than that! Over time, the financial institutions also saw this opportunity and were happy to help customers and merchants leverage the comprehensive electronic network that has been created worldwide. The first step in creating this move to electronic currency was the creation of the debit card.

Creation of the Debit Card—Paper Currency Is Now in Transition

The debit card, which in benefit, is a hybrid between your ATM card and your credit card, makes electronic purchases simple. Now you can eliminate a few steps and streamline your purchases and bank accounting. The debit card, which looks like your MasterCard or Visa credit card and is accepted all over the world (imagine that), is now being used transparently to most merchants for purchases of goods and services. Unlike when you use a check, you do not need to ask if your debit card is accepted. Just look for the MasterCard or Visa logo on the door, and you get to take advantage of this well-established credit card infrastructure.

The debit card, which is like a check except that it is plastic, automatically (via your card provider's service), takes the amount of the purchase directly out of your checking account and provides you a statement of transactions at the end of the month just like your credit card. It's almost like music how they come together with such harmony! You consumers are now responsible for making entries into a register to keep track of how much money you have in the account or you can go up to the nearest ATM machine and ask for a "Balance Enquiry." How handy! I could only imagine that with customers being so comfortable with the accuracy of bank statements over the years that some may not even keep a paper register rather just save receipts and compare them against the bank statement at the end of the month.

The acceptance and use of credit card and debit card concepts gave rise to further deployment of automated electronic access portals by merchants. The electronic portals allow customers to purchase goods and services easily, using cash or credit at the choice of the customer. Some portals specify that you manually choose cash or credit based on the type of card you insert (examples are grocery stores and gas pumps) and other portals simply debit the account number on the card. If a credit card is used, the portal charges the purchase to credit, and if a debit card is used, it takes the money from your checking account. The merchants don't care, because they have payment authorization and guarantee from the financial institution. The financial institution verifies your credit line or bank balance and returns to the merchant an authorization number. This notification authorizes your purchase or denies your purchase almost instantaneously. Now try that with a paper check—Look, Mom, no more bounced checks!

Well, not exactly, because with these evolving methods of alternative payment, you can still use them in combination to make payments. An example is your utility bill. Although automatic payment from your account is possible, some customers still like to pay with a check, because it gives them control. Vendors, unlike banks, do not have as perfect of a history accounting for the sale of goods and services. Sometimes they charge you more than you think you should pay. So we still have a way to go to get rid of all of our old banking habits and to be totally comfortable with the electronic world.

The thing I hope you see here is the fact that paper currency is not necessary for purchases in almost every major category of goods and services you make as a consumer. We simply have cash because the market is still under development and moving you to new levels of technical and practical acceptance. When it is mature, that is, ready to be used for prophetic fulfillment, it will not be hard to leverage the electronic infrastructure to control your buying of goods and services. This network fulfills this function today, just on different levels for individuals, based on their geographical locations, technical adaptation, and use of the technology.

To date, all of these technologies, including the credit card, ATM card, and debit card are dumb card technology. That is, the card has information imprinted on a magnetic strip that gives the name and account information. The card is used in conjunction with the global networking infrastructure and the financial institutions central computers to validate the account of the cardholder. It does not have any upgradeable intelligence or "read/writeable capabilities." In a sense, this is a one-way, real-time transaction model that depends on centralized clearing and authorization between the merchant and the financial institution as you purchase your goods and/or services. The merchant must be physically connected to the financial institution's computer systems to obtain the authorization. The card itself has no intelligence as to credit limits, card validation dates, and available credit; thus the merchant is dependent on this real-time connection to the financial institution that has issued the card for authorization.

The magnetic strip has been the workhorse of the financial industry, but new requirements are making this technology obsolete and giving rise to emerging chip technologies, which have been under development since the 1980s around the world. Chip technologies or the Smart Card are the future of the plastic age, giving financial institutions, merchants, and customers the ability to leverage our new global economy.

Chip Technology or "Smart Cards"—The Cornerstone of Electronic Currency

Chip technology or Smart Cards, which will be used interchangeably in this discussion, represent a new authorization model to be used by the financial industry in the near future. Unification of currency in European countries to the Euro and the rise of an electronic global marketplace requiring the need for improved security and flexibility have given rise to the continued development of this technology.

Chip technology is not new but is only recently making its debut in world markets, after much hard work, many years of development, and standardization to a global model for conducting business electronically. **Chip technology was designed from its inception to be a global interoperable model for electronic currency, providing added convenience, security, and value to the cardholder.** Financial institutions will benefit from more cost-effective transaction processing and new forms of transaction revenue, as well as abilities to offer value-added services to their merchants. Merchants will be able to create loyalty programs with their customers leveraging advanced technology to offer special discounts and purchase incentives to keep customers coming back.

Chip Technology—Banking of the Future

The authorization model will be more dynamic than that of a magnetic strip offering "off-line and on-line" intelligent transaction processing. Because the Smart Card is a microchip technology, the card has two-way capabilities, which means it can send and receive (or read and write) information as appropriate for the transaction to the respective financial institution. By design, it will always be up to date with the newest information about you, your credit availability and bank balances, your cash purse value (the cash value remaining on the card for cash type transactions), and the expiration date of the card.

The Smart Card will also have your merchant loyalty plans on the card, so that when you purchase goods and services from vendors, you can be given discounts or free merchandise to keep you coming back. If you are a traveler, your travel profiles can be kept on the card so that when you purchase tickets, you do not need to tell the ticket agent the type of seat you like and the type of room you want. And when you arrive, your electronic ticket will be on your card, so all you need to do is to insert your card at the airport gate, and off you go.

Additionally, in the future, your medical records, identification, access information to buildings, computer passwords (basically, your electronic identity) can be stored on the Smart Card and used as deemed appropriate by employers, merchants, law enforcement agencies, and computer systems—anything or anyone desiring irrefutable identification of the cardholder could benefit from this new technology.

Another major difference with this model is the ability to use the Smart Card in the exact same way as physical cash. Now you will load electronic cash value onto the card, just as you put physical cash into your wallet, pocket, or purse. Then you will then be able to use the Smart Card to purchase things from vending machines, pay for parking, or give your friend, spouse, or child cash for their needs. All of this is done electronically.

The ability to do "person-to-person" transactions is critical to the elimination of physical currency and is a major differentiator of this technology model. These transactions are done by using an "electronic purse" that lets you change your pin number for security, read your account balance(s), transfer cash from your electronic purse to someone else with an electronic purse, or upload more cash—just like you do today with physical currency. It will even have the ability to hold five different currencies in the event that you travel or live in a place that requires the use of various currencies. Now you will have no more hassles with currency exchange rates when you want to go to your local coffee shop, bakery, or the like.

Because the Smart Card has intelligence, you can conduct these financial transactions "off line," facilitating "real-world" day-to-day financial transactions used for business or personal affairs as you would today using physical currency. The next time you connect with a merchant who is "on line," a physical ATM machine, or new virtual ATM machines accessed via the telephone, Internet, or mobile phone, the Smart Card will use its microchip and audit functionality to update the respective financial institution's computers with all of the activities of your account(s).

This new model furthers the reach of electronic currency into even more areas of life, such as the transportation industry (buses and taxi cabs) and curbside merchants, because it does not require expensive "on-line" connections to financial institutions but only approved point-of-sale terminals (swipe readers or chip readers) that can hold an audit trail of transactions and electronic cash until uploaded to the merchants' or service providers' bank account when they have access to an ATM machine or other electronic banking terminals.

Smart Card Evolution

Beginning in France in the 1980s by local financial institutions, the use of Smart Cards was characterized in the early days by individual development efforts and false starts in Europe and Japan. Many major institutions began development of the technology, knowing that such change could give them a market differentiator in the already competitive world of banking. Such technology would be helpful to change the authorization models, allowing banks to reduce fraud and control bad debt, increase security, and offer value-added services to their merchants to create brand loyalty.

Changes in world economy, the development of a global electronic marketplace, the consolidation of currencies, the need to transact more business for all sizes of transactions on line, needed security improvements, person-to-person currency exchange, and rapid global expansion are all business drivers for card issuers around the world to adopt such technology.

Each player originally had its own model. Europay International used MasterCard International's model, MasterCard released Mondex on MULTOS[ii], and Visa has Visa Cash and Open Platform[iii] as their cash purse and operating system, respectively, as well as other proprietary models doing development in local markets.

As global market leaders, the major players believed that for the good of the industry, a common specification needed to be created. As a result, Europay, International, MasterCard, and Visa came together to form EMVCo, LLC in February 1999 to manage, maintain, and enhance the Europay Mastercard Visa (EMV) Integrated Circuit Card Specifications for Payment Systems as the implementation of card programs become more prevalent. Europay later merged with MasterCard in July 2002 making the shareholders of EMVCo, LLC MasterCard International and Visa International.

The importance of this new global interoperable system gave rise to defacto standards published in the form of specifications, which are being adopted today to provide a global electronic purse. In 1998 four organizations came together and formed a company called CEPSCO. The founders included Espanola A.I.E., EURO Kartensystenne, Europay International, and Visa International with early adopters—Groupement des Cartes Bancaires and Proton World. Together, they account for the majority of the world's electronic purse cards and have a strong presence in the majority of the countries where electronic purses are currently used.

Organizations from more than 22 countries, representing more than 100 million electronic purse cards, have already agreed to adopt the specifications. This means that more than 90% of the world's electronic purse cards will, in time, become interoperable.

Common Electronic Purse Specifications (CEPS), which became publicly available in March 1999, support the previously mentioned EMV specifications that define the card application, the card-to-terminal interface, the terminal application for point-of-sale and load transactions, data elements, and recommended message formats for transaction processing. In addition, CEPS also provides functional requirements for the various electronic-purse scheme participants and uses public key cryptography for enhanced security. (We will discuss more about cryptography in the security chapter).

These particulars may have more meaning for those of you in technology industry. If you are not in the industry, the previous paragraph represents the technology elements needed to develop and deploy a functional business model empowering the use of chip technology to buy and sell goods and services worldwide—as adopted by card issuers, merchants, and consumers.

Another important business issue to mention is the attention to detail given by the CEPS to leverage existing infrastructure. Because this is strategically a migration from magnetic strip to chip technology, maintaining interoperability between both models is critical. A single footprint for equipment is needed to control cost and make deployments easier. This will also make the phasing in of the technology more plausible to all participants in the industry.

The ability to leverage existing infrastructure is key for rapid adaptation and deployment globally. In order for the chip model to give financial institutions the benefits of increased revenues and controlled costs, it must be affordable to design, develop, and deploy. In my evaluation, architectural adoption of these recent defacto standards, EMV and CEPS, will indeed give financial institutions, card issuers, and merchants the tools and business justifications needed to move forward and rapidly develop and deploy this improved global electronic currency model. Consumers will benefit from the added conveniences, security, financial savings, and new features allowing for person-to-person exchange of electronic currency as easily as you can do today with physical currency.

To my excitement, my findings regarding the state of the industry pertaining to Smart Cards or chip technology was that of awe. I have been listening with one ear to the development of this technology, knowing that it would be the cornerstone and would be coming soon. But I did not, until September 2000, begin tracking its maturity and readiness. My findings were astounding! As a technologist who has been an early adopter—in other words, my theory is that you have to bleed to lead—I can tell you that we are not at the beginning of this development cycle.

This industry is mature, its leaders know how to make things happen, and they see the potential gains and understand the fierceness of global competition. The business drivers for this migration to chip technology are sound and needed, based on our current electronic global society. These financial players have aligned themselves, learning from their early mistakes, creating a global interoperable standard for chip technology, leveraging the current banking infrastructure to transact business in this brave new world. Equipment manufacturers who make the swipe readers, money collectors, and computer systems already entrenched in the support of the financial communities, are finding it easy and effective to design systems around these new standards.

Lest you wonder "How far along is far along," when manufacturers offer a variety of electronic portable point of sale terminals (swipe readers), electronic wallets (electronic purse reader), cellular phones, and yes, even key chains to read your electronic purse, "It is getting pretty real." Remember that this electronic purse concept has been under development since the 1980s and is more prevalent in markets such as Europe and Japan. Everything that early adopters tried and developed for proprietary systems is being retooled to support global standards.

There are hundreds of millions of cardholders using Smart Cards for transportation, parking, groceries, fuel, and restaurants—basically, all goods and services sectors to support life's necessities. This has proved to be a successful development environment, and future deployments and "rollouts" are now becoming more widespread, affecting many more card holders as financial institutions are more confident to launch full-scale deployment projects rather than pilot programs.

This level of maturity is critical to the successful deployment of chip technology in the United States. Because the United States represents the bulk of worldwide credit debt, we are certainly the power users of this type of technology—plastic has become part of our society! As a result, I believe that this is why, if you live in the United States, you have not seen mass deployment or even many pilots of chip technology. I do see, from time to time, offers from the major credit card players promoting such technology, but it is by no means widespread in the U.S. markets. I think there is a simple reason for this. The U.S. card market is so large that institutions have been reticent to have false starts for such programs in the United States. Because these financial organizations are worldwide, they were able to leverage their presence in other global markets where there is current market pressure for further development of electronic banking capabilities.

I am also not surprised that early adopters of chip technology are in European and Far East markets. This region of the world, along with the Middle East and Russia, are all mentioned as end time players. As a result, it is easy for me to conceive why things such as currency unification are taking place in these regions. It has been said that the Euro was impetus for development of the electronic purse standard. It created a need for cross-boarder electronic interoperability that could give card carriers the same functionality as the new physical notes that were circulated in 2002—the notes can be traded uniformly among countries in the Euro zone. Without such standardization of the electronic purse, of which there were many not interoperable in Europe, electronic currency would be more cumbersome than physical currency, and that just wouldn't work in the grand scheme of things.

Nothing happens without motives or business drivers. The evolution to a standard electronic currency model in Europe is easy to understand—it mirrors the new physical currency standardization. Propagation to other areas of the world are also easily understood with drivers like global e-commerce, the need to reduce bad debt and fraud, the desire for higher levels of security, and the ability to leverage technology to reward all participants in the form of revenue and savings, including financial institutions, merchants, and consumers.

With so many business drivers and mass markets for cardholders worldwide, it will not be long before the financial community successfully completes the migration from the magnetic strip to (micro) chip technology. As a result of this migration, which is a natural course of business evolution in the financial industry addressing today's market requirements, a technology infrastructure is in place, capable of electronically controlling a person's ability to buy and sell goods and services. This fact is critical, because without such a global infrastructure, it would be impossible to fulfill to prophecies in Revelation, Chapter 13.

Dependencies and Holdouts

The financial industry is the cornerstone of infrastructure required to have an electronic marketplace that facilitates the exchange of electronic currency worldwide for purchasing goods and services. It has been evolving for more than 30 years and has done so in response to business requirements and objectives leveraging all available emerging technologies, which have been similarly evolving in parallel in response to market pressures and industry needs, to accomplish these objectives. The financial industry will continue to rely on the security, visual media, and communications sectors to bring this financial model to complete maturity and effectiveness.

A major internal dependency and hold back of the emergence of this new financial model is global technical adaptation and use of the model by financial institutions, consumers, and merchants. This is now uniquely positioned for more widespread acceptance for the following reasons:

Financial institutions, banks or card issuers are beginning to purchase franchises for offering these services. This is because of the defacto standard that has emerged, allowing for cost- effective integration into their existing infrastructures. Acceptance of the EMV and CEPS specifications are far reaching (90% of the 100 million cards were issued during early adoption) with coverage in most markets worldwide.

Card issuers will be able to offer to their merchants new loyalty programs that will help increase the merchants' revenue by improved and sustained customer loyalty. There is also a major motive to accept this model to help reduce operating costs for networking infrastructure as well as to reduce fraud and bad debt by having improved security and more closely monitored credit limit management for cardholders.

It is also anticipated, that as digital markets emerge these are; e-commerce on the Internet, m-commerce or mobile Internet, and digital TV), additional business opportunities will develop that can take advantage of Smart Card technology, creating additional banking revenues.

Merchants will respond to customer pressure placed on them to offer Smart Card services. This is as much fear of loss as it is factual, but nonetheless, as merchants see more customers carrying these cards and asking about loyalty programs, the merchants will fall in line!

The EMV and CEPS specifications will make it easier for merchants to develop systems to transact business using the new model as well as to preserve much of their existing infrastructure investment. The merchants are generally caught in the middle between what banks are promoting as the "new way of the future" and the merchant's customers, who are responding to the card issuer's offer to adopt Smart Card technology.

Adoption for the consumer, I believe, will be the easiest part of this equation. It can happen in a variety of ways. The first and simplest is just sending a new card with the embedded technology and the old magnetic strip to the customer and then educating them on the advantages of finding merchants that accept chip technology. The customer will not be inconvenienced by the card not being accepted as usual, but may become frustrated with a merchant who is not offering the expected loyalty programs, and thus the cycle begins.

Cardholders will also be able to be motivated to accept special offers and learn new banking practices by special interest reduction or currency exchange offers. This will be very easy, particularly in the United States, as we are heavily burdened with debt. This method is really simple and effective. It saves you money on your current debt payments by substantially lowering your monthly payments. Just watch, and you will see "0%" offers, reduced interest, and improved exchange rates (if you are in an area with multiple currencies). And you can bet that customers will accept these generous offers. Just think. My banker is going to lower my payments, give me better security, save me money when shopping, allow me to purchase safely on the Internet, and maintain convenient personal profiles to save me time when booking travel. Now who in their right mind would turn down such an offer? I wouldn't, would you?

External dependencies are limited and will predominately improve what is currently being developed in the areas of security, revenue channels, and connectivity, or communications.

Security, which will be discussed in the next chapter, will continue to address the growing need for ease of use, confidence levels, and irrefutable identification of the user, proving his or her digital or computer identity as well as physical identity.

Revenue channels, which represent various forms of electronic portals for the ability to trade goods and services, will continue to improve including additional locations of point-of-sale devices (places to use your plastic card), the Internet via computer and TV as they converge (which will be discussed more in the Visual Media chapter), and mobile commerce (m-commerce), which is wireless telephone access to the Internet adding the additional feature of GPS which can be leveraged for personalized offers and enhanced services. We will look closely at m-commerce in the communications chapter, along with other forms of communications responsible for connecting users to the Internet. This is called the "last mile," which continues to be a major inhibitor for rapid global deployment of e-commerce services.

Based on the above dependencies and interdependencies with other industries, I do not see banking restricted in their ability to deploy the new chip "Smart Card" model. Their current choices for defacto standards will allow them to take advantage of improved marketing channels, security methods, and emerging wireless communications technologies engineered to globally reach consumers and eliminate last mile constraints.

You can expect to see offers in the mail for Smart Cards all around the world with deployments taking place as fast as franchises can develop their new systems and rollout services. I believe substantial growth will occur in the years 2002 through 2010 with this emerging as the new banking model, eliminating magnetic strip technology. This will happen because of all the benefits that chip technology can bring to the entire supply chain, including financial institutions, merchants, and consumers.

Notes:

[i] "Never leave home without it" is a marketing phrase for American Express, and "For everything else, there is MasterCard" is a marketing tag used by MasterCard.

[ii] MULTOS is the open operating system developed and used by Mondex International to allow application development interoperability of its Smart Cards.

[iii] Open Platform is the open operating system developed and used by Visa to allow application development and interoperability of Visa Smart Cards.

Chapter Three

The Security Industry

The Evolution of the Security Industry

In this section, we will review the evolution of security relevant to e-commerce and the development of a cashless society. It will focus on migration to methods and practices that will provide users with an irrefutable digital identity that will be used to purchase goods and services, as well as to gain access to computer systems and buildings. Your digital identity, or electronic identity, will become of great importance to you as e-commerce and new banking models using chip technology begin to emerge.

Before we begin the discussion of emerging security technologies, which will enable improved protection of your digital identity, we must first consider the broader picture of security and physical issues pertaining to it. This will give us common ground for understanding the perceptions that are driving today's developments of this industry.

Security and the concept of protecting ourselves from personal harm and our possessions from loss is age old. As long as there has been evil in the world—which has been a long, long time—we have been concerned with security. People endeavor to keep themselves out of harm's way as well as to protect their property, so that they will not feel the violation that comes from an action that would create personal harm, vandalism, theft, or war, leading to a loss of personal property.

Security principals take on many forms and generally play together, with increasing inconvenience as the level of security gets higher or tighter. Higher or tighter security levels intimates that you and your possessions are more protected from loss. The essence of security is hiding and/or locking things of value so that others may not see them, take them, or harm you or your family. This is where phrases like "out of sight, out of mind" came from.

Examples of security for your physical well being include many components:

Organized security. You trust in the government or law-enforcement agencies to protect you from physical harm by imposed laws, the legal system, and armed protection. This also includes the military, which protects our borders and keeps us safe from other countries attacking for military reasons.

Personal security. This includes having a place to live that offers security from the elements and personal harm. Personal security generally involves having a door to lock to keep people out of your home unless they are invited. It could also include alarm systems, security guards, gates, and fences to keep people off of your property or out of your neighborhood. You might pull your blinds so that people cannot look in and see what you are doing (hiding element). Depending on your station in life, you may require much more elaborate methods, including bodyguards. In practice, the more you have to lose or your role in society may heighten the amount of personal security measures you may take to protect yourself and your family from loss, harassment, or harm.

Personal property is protected in much the same way, by hiding and locking. Most people store their personal effects in their home, but that depends on the type of possessions they own. You may choose to have a safe or firebox for valuables like jewelry or important papers to make it more difficult for a thief to steal if someone breaks into your home. A safe or firebox could also protect your valuables from fire in the event of an accident.

You may also choose to store some of your valuables in another more appropriate location, depending on the asset. It could be a bank's safety deposit box or a storage yard for larger assets. Your goal in selecting a location is that the environment is safe and secured using best practices including gates, locks, guards, and video surveillance. The type of asset you are protecting and the dollars you can afford to protect these assets typically drive the location and level of security selected.

Service organizations also have responsibility to protect your identity and personal information when providing services to you. This introduces the notion of confidentiality. That is, the service received from the service agency is to remain private as appropriate to the type of service rendered and the respective nature of the transaction. If it is your medical records, these are to remain private unless you release access to these records to other heath care providers. If it is your financial information, this is to remain private from the public. If it real estate transaction, this is public information. Hence, some information is visible in what is called "Public Record" (if you live in the United States).

Before the invention of computer systems and electronic data processing technology, which occurred in the mid-1900s, much of the safekeeping of records was done by hand on paper records. Business processes and laws were put in place to assure confidentiality of private matters and to define what needs to be public. Agreements or contracts with organizations were physically signed and witnessed with a "notary public" acting as a non-biased third party. The notary, as part of his or her responsibility, would validate your identity by physically evaluating your identification such as a driver's license or passport, then would witness your signature on the respective document and place his or her signature and seal of authority on the document beside your signature. This process in our legal system was accepted as a way to assure an irrefutable signature authority on a legal document. The requirement for a "notarized signature" is generally attached to something of legal significance such as financial documents for loans, court actions, and legal settlements, and power of attorney, which gives someone else your signature authority.

To become a notary public, you would apply for such a responsibility, agree to perform the job, and keep records as required by the position. The notary understood that his or her records could be audited and that he or she could be called upon in a court of law to witness that a person did sign a document in his or her presence. Finding this trusted third-party signature authority has been as simple as going down to your local bank or other public office or your attorney's office.

This process has been going on for years, but the times change our requirements. The world, as a result of the transportation and electronic revolution, has become a much faster and smaller place. Business, which in the past was conducted locally in a geographic area with local vendors, is now expanded around the country and even the world. This created a need to find new ways to communicate and authorized transactions faster, because after all, "Time is money." The traditional mail system was the first to change, with the advent of overnight mail. Federal Express created a revolution and became a household name overnight. Have you ever heard the phase, "Just

FedEx it"? This was so common and became so synonymous with overnight mail that the company's name was later changed to FedEx Corporation.

Overnight mail helped speed information around the world for years and became a profitable industry for the shipping business. But as with all good things, we still must get better and faster so that we can "spend more time with our families." No, so that we can get better and faster.

Well, somewhere along the way, an electronic industry started to develop to close the gap on time and create an even more instantaneous method of conducting business around the corner or across the world. Varieties of digital technology were emerging to help conduct business faster, more efficiently, and with fewer time constraints. Things like the fax machine, voice mail, and e-mail were developed, leveraging vast networks of telephone and data connectivity that were quickly becoming known as the information super highway.

Businesses and consumers had already become familiar with the power of the telephone, which, with its almost global reach, virtually changed the world. And with tags such as "It's the next best thing to being there,"[iv] a long-distance call was reliable and, in comparison to travel, inexpensive.

Computer networks connecting the world were also being developed with the advent of the Internet.

Used first for the military and later for academia, this sprawling network of computers connected educational institutions around the world together with a common backbone and computer protocol (or computer language), allowing them to share information and send e-mail among those on this network. This network would later become the impetus for a craze in electronic global commerce and knowledge exchange second to none. As a result, it changed our world forever.

These two infrastructures–for telephone (voice) and computing (data)–began to develop separately with the inevitable future event looming–the convergence of the two to create a cohesive information highway.

The fax machine was the first major craze, because it fit so well into our current business processes. There was nothing new here. You simply produced your document and then placed it into a machine that would send it over the telephone line to another machine that could speak "fax," and within minutes, your associate was looking at what you had just written. What a powerful tool. Now we no longer need to wait for that overnight document to come so that we can edit a document and come to agreement on the contents of the document. This was indeed revolutionary, and it spread like wildfire around the world. This tool was used for years in the business marketplace and is still being used today because of its simplicity and effectiveness.

The fax machine, which leveraged the existing telephone or voice network, saved companies thousands of dollars in overnight shipping, as well as time, "which is money." It also helped with time constraints as companies began to trade overseas with world markets. You could work on the information during the day and then send the document. It would be available to your counterpart when he or she walked into the office. What a concept!

Eventually, the dependability and popularity of the fax machine gave rise to using this tool as an acceptable method to enter into business agreements with companies. At first it became a defacto standard business practice. That is, companies agreed to accept and people agreed to let this electronic instrument bind them in a business transaction. It was typically the same type of document you would physically sign and send to enter into a business relationship, such as a contract or purchase order.

As with all technical adaptation, market pressure begins to move behavior and practices. Over time, mass acceptance and use of this electronic method to transmit physical documents created the laws necessary to support this first generation of digital signature. Now legal documents can be faxed and are binding in a court of law. This was the first practical step in the evolution of digital signature, which will be one of the major points of this chapter and a key component in the discussion of digital (or computer) security necessary for e-commerce.

Voice mail arrived on the scene in the middle 1980s and eventually changed how businesses would communicate. The notion, especially with the world seeming to become a smaller place and the need for communication across time zones, was that much of what we needed to say could be done in a "non real-time" mode. In other words, you could accomplish more, in many cases, by just sending your message requesting the answer needed. You would do this at your convenience, and it could be picked up at the called party's convenience, regardless of time.

This had much push back for adaptation in the community, especially in the area of "Automated Attendant," which was a by-product of this technology. The automated attendant would offer callers choices of how to direct their own calls, saving the company money in secretarial staffing costs. I remember the pitch well, as I sold many of these systems. The system never sleeps, doesn't have a bad day, never takes a day off, doesn't require a raise, and never takes a lunch break. Every benefit an employer could ever dream of–the perfect employee! This was used as part of the "hard dollar" justification for the purchase of such as system. The rest is history. Just pick up the phone and call a major service organization.

This was one of the first technologies used to create a "self-help" environment. It grew in popularity, offering information on line via voice announcements. It later converged the already popular fax machine into the equation by allowing callers to request that forms or instructions be sent to their fax machine automatically to meet their business needs. This would later give rise to the Internet web page for the next generation of on-line, self-help services.

During this discussion, keep your mind on the parallel development of these industries supporting voice and data functionality. Notice how they connect into each other and fuel development and unification of these technologies to provide a cohesive means to communicate and conduct business globally.

Also in the mid 1980s, the PC began to emerge in the office landscape. The personal computer, with its open standards and relatively low cost (in comparison to mainframe computing) started to take off. I will not focus on this, but its success goes without saying. All you need to do is look around in business and your home—computers are everywhere. The industry is even trying to converge computers into your television allowing you to purchase on line and send e-mail (we will discuss more about this in the visual media chapter). The focus for this discussion, relevant to security, is the computers' influence that created the demand for e-mail and on-line purchases.

The acceptance and use of the fax machine and voice mail exposed additional electronic needs for communication functionality. Documents that were created on this new powerful invention, the PC, needed to be "attached and sent" to people so that they could work on the document. After all, we have become accustomed to this with the fax machine. So of course we would expect the same thing from our PC. But this was not, initially, the case. A user would compose the document, print the document, and then fax it for review. Or if the user was in the office, he or she would copy it to a disk and carry it over to his or her counterpart so that it could be electronically edited.

I am sure that by now you are getting the picture. Why would we need to create a physical printout of an electronic document so that it can be sent electronically via fax? Or why would we need to copy this onto a disk to be able to work on it with another PC? Because the network or LAN had not yet been created and popularly adopted. This too became history as the PC became connected first to the other machines in the office and then to machines all over the world.

E-mail, which had been used on the Internet long before it became popular in the office, started to emerge. This tool first allowed users to send documents created on their PCs as attachments to other users in their office. Later attachments could be sent around the country or the world, leveraging the company's private network and then via the

Internet to other organizations that were connected to the information highway.

Software manufacturers created tools that unified the management of information so that users could handle voice mail, faxes, and e-mail with equal functionality. This unified messaging concept, which started in the late 1980s, continues to develop today and is rising in popularity because we are dialogued (flooded) with information from all sources, as not one of these communication methods has become pervasive. Each has its place, characteristics, and levels of adaptation. So to varying degrees, we must manage all of these forms of communication as effectively and securely as possible.

E-mail, like the fax, has become important and even critical to conducting business, because of its greater functionality and timesaving attributes. It has revolutionized how companies do business with one another in this global economy, creating a virtual culture. Now with this tool and connectivity to the Internet, you can be having a conversation on the telephone, send a document to be reviewed in seconds, edit the document on line as you speak to one another, and then forward the document to the needed parties for authorization and acceptance.

This has changed forever how we conduct business. The efficiency of e-mail has created market pressure from businesses and lawmakers to approve methods for e-mail to be legally binding, similar to what happened with the fax machine. And with the fax machine, businesses currently accept a validated electronic signature or an e-mail transmission in acceptance of a contract as binding for many business transactions. This has worked primarily for purchases, as vendors are always interested in figuring out a way to more easily get you to spend money for their goods and services.

This, however, has not been as easy for legally binding documents or information of a confidential nature, because of the non-secure nature of the Internet. All transmissions of data–including the content of documents, their origin, and their destination–can be viewed with test equipment designed to analyze and test the network. These are called sniffers or protocol analyzers. Without spending a lifetime discussing how data packets move, let's just say that when you are ready to send your document, it is put in a packet or a sort of electronic envelope. Systems (routers and gateways) along the way need the ability to read the "To address" and the "From address" to deliver the package. This is analogous to the physical mail system, which uses the "To address" to complete delivery or the "From address" to return undeliverable packages to the originating sender.

Most of the routing systems do not need to open the envelope and see what is inside (contents) to get the packet delivered, just like your local mailman. But there are times in the data world that for reasons of security, advanced routing, espionages, or electronic theft, a person (using a protocol analyzer) or a system cracks open the packet and views its contents.

As a result of this known fact, methods of security were created to do the basics discussed earlier in the chapter–to "lock and hide" the contents of the packet so that it can only be read and used by the intended parties. This is known as cryptology and digital authentication.

The use of cryptology and digital authentication is the foundation for creating your digital identity of the future. It is critical for you to understand your digital identity (or computer or electronic identity), because it is relevant to the emergence of a cashless, electronic, global marketplace.

Electronic security, which includes cryptology that is used to "hide" information and digital authentication that is used to "lock and unlock" information is driven by the same basic motive as all security methods—fear of loss.

The security industry, for the purposes of this chapter, will include all of the respective industry sectors responsible for developing electronic security solutions, including:

- Firewalls–which keep people out of your network and hide network elements
- Cryptology–which hides the data contents being transmitted via the network

- Authentication—which provides access to systems and validates your identity (to various degrees, based on the method used)
- Digital Signature—which is a computer signature that is legally binding for purchases and documents.

These elements comprise the foundation of electronic security, which are access control, identification, and encryption.

The security industry began by serving the military and government security sectors. It advanced over time into a cat and mouse game with our enemies. The security industry worked toward providing the United States with methods of hiding and locking information so that our adversaries could not steal these secrets and benefit from the discovery of the contents of the transmission. This happened on all communications fronts, including voice, data, and video-type transmissions.

I could spend a great deal of time discussing security, but I am not writing a primer on security technology. Rather, I desire for you to see the practical and parallel evolution of these industries and how they are dependent on one another to further the practical benefit and acceptance of the respective technologies in the big scheme of things.

All of our military and national security efforts have created a very usable and secure (or virtually un-crackable) "security model" that is being used today to address our needs for digital security and to create a digital identity.

Companies are benefiting from advance firewall technologies, which keep hackers out of their businesses. The highest methods of encryption used today have not been cracked or violated, and new methods of authentication used to sign you onto systems with a unique password each time are improving access control to computer systems worldwide.

Additional technologies, which support the concept of digital signature, are also emerging and being used worldwide in deployments. Public Key Infrastructure (PKI) is a method that uses an independent third party or certificate authority, which validates the identity of the users and the systems that are being using for the transaction. This method, which blends authentication and encryption together, is addressing the global need to have this level of security without the need to distribute to people another physical device (Token) used to generate a unique password for access to computer systems.

A Token (looks like a calculator with a window showing a number and sometimes a keypad to enter numbers): Tokens are used by corporate networks to provide this function, are expensive and cumbersome to use, and are not conducive to mass distribution and distributed computing. The Internet is a distributed computing model, which means that information is connected with pages that have links. These links can lead anywhere, including different locations—hence, they are distributed rather than centralized.

PKI, with its ability to address security requirements in a geographically distributed computing environment, has become the choice and method of many key "secure protocols" used in Internet applications. Some of these protocols are Secure Sockets Layer (SSL), Secure/Multimedia Internet (S/MIME), and Secure Electronic Transactions (SET), and code signing services for both Java and ActiveX. All of these specify the use of PKI as the secure authentication model. Some of this terminology may be unfamiliar to those of you who are not in technology, but to those of us who are, it represents the most commonly used protocols and programming languages used for developing Internet applications and securing them.

PKI depends on a number of pieces to complete the authorization function, including the certificate authority, certificates, and public and private keys. These all work together to assure the validity of a person's digital signature, protect the identities of the parties and the contents of the transmissions, and grant authorization to the needed computer systems so that the information can be accessed.

The certificate authority (CA) is a third party who is required to administer the certificates to the requesting parties. Part of the job of the CA is to validate the identity of the person or machine before it issues a certificate, which will be trusted by other persons and systems using this security model. It is much like a "notary public," as discussed earlier. The CA uses best practices to determine your identity, such as checking your passport or driver's license. It knows personal things about you, based on information that you provide in response to the CA verification process. The detail of verification will be determined by the level of security needed by the application and the agreement(s) in place with the provider(s) of information and services. The CA can be an independent, third party service such as VeriSign, offering services to any entity requiring the use of PKI security methods, or the company or institution providing access to electronic content can handle CA internally.

Certificates, which are issued by the CA, are, in effect, your digital signature or electronic fingerprint. This certificate, like your fingerprint, is unique, and based on your request for this certificate it represents your authority, just like your signature, when you attach this to an electronic transaction requiring a secure, irrefutable, verified digital signature. When you initiate a transaction using software on your computer, a Smart Card or any Internet enabled device designed to conduct business electronically, that device will use embedded security software designed to generate a public and/or private key and bond your digital certificate (or signature) to the key and send it to the intended party for processing.

Public key, which is part of the technology's name, is the locking and hiding part of this security model. Keys are issued in pairs to parties so that information can be locked on the originating end by the sending party and opened on the receiving end by the intended receiving party.

A user may have a number of key pairs. For example, you may have a pair of keys for your signature and a pair of keys to encrypt (or hide) the contents of your data transmission. Keys must be managed just as you manage keys today with a physical lock. If you lose your keys, you cannot gain access to the locked area.

In the digital world, because of encryption methods, this is very important to understand. Because unlike a physical door, which, when keys are lost, you can call a locksmith to make a new key, you cannot create a new digital key to access previously locked information. As a result, the data transmitted with the lost keys cannot be recovered unless the lost keys can be reduplicated. This creates a requirement for providers of services and users of services to keep a backup copy of their digital keys. This is done on a disk or separate computer. Businesses and institutions using PKI will also have key assignment, revocation, backup, and recovery processes in place to serve as an electronic locksmith.

This security infrastructure is being embraced by the e-commerce world because it is perfectly suited to be used for Internet-type business transactions. Its lack of global deployment has been partially due to the complexity and expense of such an implementation, as you may deduce from the description above. In addition, businesses have been reticent to deploy technology until a defacto standard emerges that would provide some measure of legal protection relevant to electronic signature and contract enforcement when purchasing goods and services. To date, there is a tremendous amount of lost revenue from contesting purchases on the Internet. If a customer says he or she didn't authorize the purchase of something, then companies must write off the charge, because they do not have irrefutable proof of the person's electronic identity.

This is now about to change worldwide because of recent laws that have been passed all over the world which make electronic signature legally binding. On October 1, 2000, the United States passed the Electronic Signatures in Global and National E-Commerce Act (E-Sign). On December 13, 1999, the European Union mandated that all countries in Europe be prepared to comply by July 2001 with a regulation that gives an electronic signature the same legal weight as a "handwritten" signature. In Asia, the impetuous for digital signature is being spearheaded by the commercial sector to help streamline paperwork for interregional trade. Their first digital contract was signed on September 25,

2000, between a local company and one in Japan. Other nations including Malaysia, South Korea, and Singapore already have digital signature laws in place. Japan is planning to give full government enforcement by the end of 2001. [v]

These recent laws and movements around the world to make digital signature legal and enforceable in a court of law will give businesses the drivers they need to begin to mass deploy this type of technology worldwide. This is an important concept, because it is attached to many business drivers, which primarily focus on the money. The new laws will help to reduce fraud and write-offs from the denial of purchases, and to increase revenue by stimulating international trade while simultaneously increasing customer confidence concerning buying on line by eliminating the fear of loss.

With laws, security standards, and defacto standards in place, businesses and institutions that can benefit from transacting business electronically will commence their march to leveraging the benefits of this global business marketplace. The key to the success of this model is simplicity. Unfortunately, simplicity is typically in direct conflict with high security. There has always been a trade-off in the security industry between convenience and security. The more convenient, the less secure, and vice versa.

The future of e-commerce and digital signature or "digital identity," based on the laws that are being passed around the world, necessitates a very high level of security to assure consumer and business confidence. So the question becomes: How will industry provide this new, high level of security while making it easy for people to use so that it can be rapidly adopted worldwide for maximum benefits by all?

The answer lies in the wings, but I have some ideas. First, I think that companies providing goods and services will focus on ways to most inexpensively leverage digital signature and new secure on-line payment models. The reason for this is simple— Information Technology (IT) departments are currently taxed with rising costs and the need to do more with less people. The thought of deploying a massive new security infrastructure internally may be less appealing in today's economic climate, not to mention that the new security model's basic design requires a trusted third party to provide the validation of identity. So why not outsource some of these functions?

I believe businesses will look to and leverage the financial industry and their current migration to chip technology to leverage maximum benefit from this new electronic frontier. After all, to transact business electronically on the web, you must use some form of plastic—like a credit, debit, or Smart Card to complete the purchase. This would "kill two birds with one stone." Now customers will get the security they need to transmit their financial information on line, and businesses will have the customer's digital signature, which is legally binding for the transaction. This is a match made in Heaven, so to speak, and, as with all great sweeping technology migrations, is a circular feeding frenzy.

All We Like Sheep

Banks, of course, want adoption of this new chip technology, which we discussed in the financial chapter. Customers need higher levels of security to create confidence for on-line purchases, which fueled the development of Smart Cards that have higher levels of security. Businesses will now begin to require, based on recently passed laws, a digital signature along with the transaction. Customers will try to find a simple way to obtain a digital signature. And lo and behold, our trusted and helpful banker is going to leverage his new chip technology model, which already uses Public Key Infrastructure security methods to easily provide you with the needed digital certificate to transact business on line.

Just think, with this new, handy, dandy, chip-powered plastic, you will be able to purchase and sign with one simple card! Wow, what a plan. Now all you need to do is to watch the mail for your new toaster, because you have just been moved again to exactly where you need to be to play in this new global electronic marketplace. So how does it make you feel to think that we like sheep can be so simply led to exactly where we need to be to function in our new global neighborhood.

So what's next? After all, this looks pretty perfect. You are now a player in the big game, and business and financial institutions have what they need to minimize risk and increase revenues. Life is good, right? Wrong.

This is a positioning step to the bigger picture, which will come with a similar strategy moving you to the next step, based on a complex, parallel series of events that make you think that everything being done is in your best interest. After all, we cannot violate our civil liberties of privacy by making such things mandatory. It is much easier if this type of thing is your idea.

By the way, I am not paranoid, nor do I care about the idea of big brother watching us. I simply believe that all that is happening is being directed by a much higher power and is strategically being done to fulfill God's ultimate plan for the world. This plan is to establish His reign on Earth, creating a new Heaven and Earth so that we can live together in harmony and experience the life that He originally intended for us to have. This life is without pain, sickness, sorrow, poverty, or confusion. The love of God will be present, and it will never be dark, because His glory will be the eternal light. People will enjoy the beauty and splendor of Heaven and all of the benefits of being a child of God, the greatest of which is to be with Him.

The Next Steps

Digital identity, as discussed to this point, primarily focuses on e-commerce, but it could reach farther in the very near future. Recently, and I am not going to focus on the details of this disaster out of respect for those who suffered personal losses, America suffered a great loss to the enemy of terrorism. The World Trade Towers and the Pentagon were attacked, and our nation suffered a great loss of life and a feeling of defilement regarding our personal security and safety. It has been said by many that we have entered into a new era in world history and that life, as we have known it, may never be the same.

Our nation and the world must now consider how to fight this enemy and win the war on terrorism. Unfortunately, it is likely to be a war that will go on for a long time, and it may never be won, because of the evil behind this strategy. In contrast, it could become the impetuous for events that would lead up to the initiation of a worldwide 7-year peace treaty with Israel as prophesied in the Book of Revelation. This is yet to be seen, and I am certainly not making a prediction here. Rather, I would like you to focus on the practical things that may come up relevant to security that could leverage the technology we have recently discussed.

Days after the September 11, 2001, attack, it became clear that the falsification of identification was an enabler for the terrorists to be able to hijack the four airplanes used in the attack. Cash was also found in the terrorists' possession that could be used to make untraceable purchases or to influence those from whom they were making purchases to sell the needed goods or services.

The following week, articles began to be written throughout the media discussing the need to heighten security and improve identification methods. It was suggested that there be a national identification card. Some states were discussing face-scanning equipment for photos used on driver's licenses.[vi] And similar technology has been used in public places such as San Diego's Qualcom Stadium during sporting events to scan crowds and compare face prints to the database.[vii] The bottom line is that our fear of loss of our personal safety will outweigh our desire for some civil liberties and privacy. After all, I would rather be alive–with people knowing a little, or a lot about me–than dead! How about you?

The subject of irrefutable physical identification could soon become of much greater importance to the American people and our friends around the world as we continue this war on terrorism and begin to use electronic currency. As we discuss this notion of heightened physical security, I would ask you again to turn your attention to how things fit together and are developed in parallel to create the motives needed and technologies required to promote your adaptation to the newly required security or financial model.

For example, we see that the financial industries' development and promotion of Smart Cards could prove to be an ideal tool to help provide a more verifiable identity using electronic methods. The same chip technology used to process financial information, leveraging all of the security modeling we discussed earlier in this chapter, could also contain additional personal information such as your driver's license, passport, or medical information. In addition, your travel information (such as airline tickets) could be electronically coded on the card. Now you have your digital identity in one place as well as the card acting as your boarding pass–or electronic ticket, and it uses the highest possible security available to protect your privacy. It's interesting to think about the fact that airline travel is one of the scenarios demonstrated on MasterCard's Australian web site as an emerging future application for Smart Cards.

Until recently, you might have considered this electronic identification and ticketing concept far fetched or far off in the future. Unfortunately, based on the importance of air travel and the recent fear that was stricken into the hearts of people around the world–that they could become part of a diabolical and evil plot to ride an airplane, acting as a guided missile of mass destruction, into a building–this is NOT far fetched but is very possible and could happen soon! The business drivers of convenience and novelty may not have been enough to move people to this concept, but the need for security and safety in the interest of preservation of life will!

Now let's reflect on the migration strategy. Smart Card issuers were promoting the convenience of chip technology because you did not need to provide the airlines with all of your preferences and credit card information. The airlines simply accept your Smart Card, which contains your identity and digital signature, your travel profile down to the type of seat you prefer, and then, with two-way capabilities, have your electronic ticket downloaded to your Smart Card for use at the gate. Very simple and efficient. I can't wait to have mine! Now this may have taken a great deal of time to adopt, but with recent fears and new flight safety requirements because of terrorism, this could be adopted at any time.

So this is just one scenario that may help. But it, too, even with its security and benefits, has limitations and will need to be improved over time. Improvements will be based on our knowledge of a security sector called biometrics. Biometrics is the association of something physically unique about your body, such as a fingerprint, eye print, or facial print. The technology uses a database to compare your previously stored physical attribute to that being scanned now on the biometrics security device. If everything matches, then you are given access. If not, you are denied access until your identity can be confirmed.

This technology requires a comprehensive on-line database and biometric devices to check people's physical attributes against the database. To date, this has not been deployed commonly because of the expense and complexity of the solution. It has typically been reserved for the highest levels of security found in government facilities and large corporations to protect valuable assets. We get our best glimpse of it in spy movies, in which advanced computer hackers are putting the hero's eye print into the database to be scanned and accepted to allow access to the data vault.

It is possible that we will see more biometric technologies used, partially when government agencies are involved in the identification process, because they have the technical resources and money needed to leverage this technology. But it remains an on-line technology in an "on-line and off-line" virtual and transit world. So what could become a low-cost option to provide intelligent security, which has the benefits of being physically associated with your body, and yet add even more benefits, such as the ability to know your location or the state of your health? Implants!

I believe the future of security for personal and financial identification will ultimately become a microchip implanted inside your body. Can you all hear the "twilight zone music" going off in my head? "Do, do, do, do," pause, "Do, do, do, do." Is it going off in your head? Well, it might be after we discuss how feasible this is today and how relevant it will be to end-time prophecy.

All singing aside, this theory falls right in line with what we have seen happening throughout this book. This industry, like all of the others discussed, has been in parallel development in preparation for this day for many years, and it is getting ready to take its place in history when the right series of events will launch it into prevalence.

Implant technology is not new to the world. It has been done in animal tagging for years. You can take your dog or cat to the vet and the vet will, with an injection, place under the skin a chip that has a unique identification number, the pet's name, the owner's name and address, which can be scanned using an inexpensive hand-held device to read the content of the chip.

Recent improvements and patents (patent number 5,629,678[viii]) by Applied Digital Solutions, Inc. created a miniature digital transceiver named Digital Angel™, leveraging the knowledge of a company (which Applied Digital Solutions, Inc. acquired) called Destron Fearing. Destron Fearing (now named Digital Angel™ Corporation) was a pioneer in microchip tagging of animals. This acquisition has yielded a new chip that also includes Global Positioning System (GPS) technology and can be powered by your body's own energy so that you never need to change a battery, and the chip is only about the size of grain of rice. Applied Digital Solutions, Inc. also has another solution called VeriChip™. This is a miniaturized, implantable identification technology that can be implanted today at various sites around the United States.

A press release dated October 2, 2000, gave the following background: "In December of 1999, Applied Digital Solutions announced that it had acquired the patent rights to a miniature digital transceiver—which it has named Digital Angel™. In some of its applications, the tiny device is expected to be bonded closely to the body or implanted just under the skin. The Company believes Digital Angel will be able to send and receive data and be located by GPS (Global Positioning System) technology. In addition to monitoring the location and medical condition of at-risk patients, the Company believes Digital Angel could have other applications that will prove to be extremely popular in the marketplace. These applications include locating lost or missing individuals or household pets; tracking endangered wildlife; managing livestock and other far-related animals; pinpointing the location of valuable stolen property; finding lost airline baggage and postal packages; managing the commodity supply chain; preventing the unauthorized use of firearms; and providing a tamper-proof means of identification for enhanced e-commerce security."

As you read press releases published by Applied Digital Solutions, Inc. you can see that they have their eyes focused on this $100 billion industry and are promoting it for the "good and welfare of mankind." Their concept is that the chip, which was first placed in watches and pagers because that is more socially acceptable, would allow you to monitor the whereabouts of a person that may have wandered off or who has become lost or kidnapped. It also gives you the ability to monitor their vital signs, such as pulse, body temperature, electrocardiogram or (EKG) and report back to a physician who is responsible for monitoring the patient's condition. The implications of being able to have a tamper-proof method of identification for e-commerce could not have been conceived at a more appropriate time. These concepts and everything going into the development of this product offering will fit nicely into what we are going to need for the future, based on impending events. Most recently, Applied Digital announced in October 2004, that VeriChip, the world's first implantable radio frequency identification (RFID) microchip for human use, has been cleared by the U.S. Food and Drug Administration (FDA) for medical uses in the United States.[ix]

Our need for adopting implant technology will again revolve around issues of self—particularly the need for personal and financial security. We will see the need to merge standards-based chip technology (Smart Cards) used in banking with the irrefutable identification capabilities of implanted devices. This marriage will make perfect sense, providing consumers with a solution to the impending security challenges of Smart Cards, as well as providing proper identification for world travel because of the rise in international terrorism.

Security Challenges for Smart Cards

Smart Cards, by their design, have embedded security mechanisms incorporated as part of their use, as discussed in the financial chapter. Smart Cards are designed to protect by encryption (hiding) the electronic identity of the user, as information is transmitted to the electronic marketplace for purchases of goods and services. One problem that will emerge is the issue of a lost or stolen card. If a card is lost or stolen it is just like money. If you have money on your card, it, too, is lost forever, just as if you had lost the physical cash in your wallet. The card also requires the use of a pin number (your secret code), and with such a number, the card can be used anywhere by anyone without the need for a physical matching signature—as the signature authority is now digital and assumed authentic by its very design and security methodologies. It is situations like these, as well as increased occurrences of digital identity crimes, that will drive people to consider the use of implant technologies.

With an implant, you will have an irrefutable, physically associated, electronic identity, which can be used to identify you to governments, businesses, airlines, and banks, as well as to facilitate secure electronic financial transactions. Wide use of this technology will be positioned to promote greater levels of personal safety from emerging world threats, as well as offering a simple, convenient method for accessing the global electronic marketplace as your monies can be downloaded into the chip that resides in your hand or forehead instead of your plastic Smart Card. The direct benefit is that no one can physically steal your card, nor can it become lost or misplaced. This gives new meaning to the phrase "I would lose my head if it wasn't attached."

In case you are wondering why I would say the chip would be placed in your hand or forehead, let me explain technically and then prophetically:

First, from a practical situation, the chip is a low-power transmitter, so the closer to the surface the better, as you want as little interference (with clothes) as possible with the transmission.

Second, you need to be able to easily position the implanted chip near the "chip reader" to complete purchases or to identify yourself. A standard insertion point for the chip makes it easier to design systems, as well as to leverage normally exposed and movable parts of the human anatomy.

Third, some technologies require the placement of the implant in the "thin and capillary-rich part of the hand and forehead to provide the necessary energy exchange to make the chip "self powered."

Fourth, it is an imitation of the seal that God will place on the forehead of believers in the Tribulation (Revelation 7:3). Satan often copies the things of God.

Fifth, the Bible prophetically says:

"He (the false prophet acting in the interest of the antichrist)[x] also forced everyone, small and great, rich and poor, free and slave, to receive a mark on his right hand or on his forehead, so that no one could buy or sell unless he had the mark, which is the name of the beast or the number of his name. This calls for wisdom. If anyone has insight, let him calculate the number of the beast, for it is man's number. His number is 666." (Revelation 13:16-18).

This placement is simply a fulfillment of prophecy as God's word has foretold for 2000 years. In my mind, this simple, literal, prediction of things to come makes it easier for us to watch for the evolution of such a requirement and safeguard ourselves from being deceived at the time it happens.

I could belabor this point or make it more sensational, but I won't, because I know it will get plenty of coverage in days to come. I will ask you, however, to please watch carefully the evolution of the things I have discussed in these chapters. Events could look different and there may be other issues developing that could drive us to acceptance, but the bottom line is that we will move to a security process like this that will allow for the irrefutable identification and secured access to the global electronic marketplace.

It is at this time that you will know that the infrastructure is right from a functional and security perspective to facilitate the Antichrist's false prophet to fulfill prophecy and impose this global mandate on mankind. All of the technology presented in the last two chapters will be tools used to make this possible. At no other time in the history of man could such a prophecy be fulfilled—we are watching the end of the age unfold before our eyes. Jesus is coming, and He says He will come like "a thief in the night." Are you ready, or will He surprise you?

I hope my presentation of this content and message will motivate you to never look at your credit card, a card reader, an e-ticket, or the sale or purchase of anything the same way ever again. My prayer is that the evolution of these events will be a constant reminder to you that Jesus is coming and that you need to be prepared to meet him regardless of the hour of his coming—because no man knows the day or the hour except God the Father.

Dependencies and Holdouts

The security industry, with the development of methods to protect consumers and businesses while conducting business electronically, is a key enabler to the expansion of the infrastructure and the adoption of e-commerce worldwide. The security industry supports the financial industry, as well as expanding the markets of other technology sectors like visual media and communications, which we will discuss in upcoming chapters.

To date, there are few technical holdbacks to the most basic elements of electronic security, which is the ability to lock and hide information. Encryption (hiding) and authentication (locking) methods for Internet or Web enabled applications have matured to a place where they can be used by businesses globally to secure their business applications. The use of Public Key Infrastructure and secure communication protocols can give customers and businesses the protection they need to do business over a global e-commerce network including all types of access portals. Remember, an access portal is anything you use to conduct business electronically—for example, it could be a swipe reader, a TV, a computer, or a cell phone.

The industry stands ready with implant technology to advance consumers to the next level after they begin to use and enjoy the successes of the new Smart Cards but experience loss from physical issues, such as cards being lost or stolen. Implants exist today and have proven history in animals, as well as in people. Advance patents will simply make the technology better and smaller for the future. Such technology will act as a means of converging identification and financial requirements into one irrefutable and cost-effective solution for global mass deployment.

Dependencies are more tied to the global deployment of the new Smart Cards chip model in replacement of the magnetic strip model that currently is prevalent in the financial community.

I believe, based on accepted global standards or specifications such as the EMV and CEPS (see the financial chapter for more information) and the business drivers behind banks adopting this new model, that it is just a matter of time before you begin to see mass deployments. Deployments will likely start in Europe, Asia, Japan and Australia because Smart Cards are in use there now. Then the Smart Cards chip model will expands to other world markets, including the United States market.

You will not likely see the use of implant technology until the financial community has globally deployed the new chip model for e-commerce. I don't think that the need for electronic identification because of public safety issues would drive people or governments to mandate the use of the technology independent of the financial element. Time will tell. The outcome will depend on the level of fear generated by the war on terrorism.

Holdouts are really more logistical because of the expense and complexities of implementing these new security models. Implementations require money, time, and motive on the part of businesses and the financial community. Recent technical and financial standards, and legal precedence worldwide, are starting to fuel the fire of companies' business cases to adopt and deploy such technologies to truly take advantage of the electronic revolution.

Simplicity will be the key issue in the deployment of digital security, as consumers will fight hard or push back on using electronic methods if they are complicated or difficult. It is for this reason that I think the responsibility will fall on the financial community to make it as simple to use as our current plastic card of choice. When this happens, it will be just a matter of time before the way we purchase goods and services will change forever. And based on "How time flies," I don't think we are going to need to wait too long!

Technically, this is one of the most critical chapters of the book to understand, because it is the culmination of many technologies and will be the one that touches our lives—most literally. I do not know when we will see or experience this, but I know the day will come when we are given a choice to accept the mark of the Antichrist or reject him and the world system of the day—meaning you will be unable to buy or sell goods or services. It is imperative that you do not choose to accept this mark at the time you are given such an ultimatum, no matter how dark or dismal things may seem.

The Bible says that taking the mark represents your eternal separation from God and Jesus Christ and that it will bring upon you the full wrath of God's judgment.

There is no easy way to say this—the grace of the message is that God has foretold us of this day in the Bible, which is His living Word, so that we can be prepared for the things to come. My heart is to see you ready for the return of Jesus Christ so that you can experience the fullness of God's love and His plan for your life both now on Earth and in the eternity to come.

Notes:

[iv] Used by AT&T during long distance advertisements.
[v] *NetworkWorldFusion* article published October 2, 2000.
[vi] *The Denver Post,* September 19, 2001.
[vii] *Newsweek Magazine*, September 24, 2001.
[viii] *Applied Digital Solutions Inc.,* April 22, 2004, http://www.adsx.com/prodservpart/patentsproprietary.html
[ix] *Applied Digital Solutions Inc.* press release dated October 13, 2004. FDA Clears VeriChip for Medical Applications in the United States.
[x] Words in parentheses were added by the author for context.

Chapter Four

The Visual Media Industries

The Evolution of Visual Media Convergence

In this section, we will review the evolution of the visual media industries relevant to e-commerce and the development of a cashless society and a global community. We will focus on the convergence of various visual medias including TV, the Internet, the entertainment industry, and the financial community. We will look at how the importance of providing visual content to consumers has facilitated the involvement of other industry sectors, such as the security, financial, and communication industries to prepare this important technology for its place in history to enable the fulfillment of end-time prophecies.

Before we discuss the various participants and their roles in the visual media, let's put a few things in context. First, let's define convergence as it relates to this section. Convergence is the blending of various technologies and business processes together to provide improved results when offering products, services, and information to your audience. In this case, it is the blending of multimedia communication tools that are visual and audible in nature, which means that they appeal to your sense of sight and hearing. Sight is an important sense, and it is said that 68 percent of communication comes by sight. That is, we rely on what we see and our ability to interpret body language to validate that which we may hear in discussion. This was a key driver for the development of such technologies as video conferencing and streaming video (*one way* video broadcasts that are "streamed" down the Internet to your computer) as businesses found that to communicate effectively in remote meetings, you need to be able to see one another.

You will see how the popularity, power, and penetration of TV: the global expansion of the Internet and its ability to provide content and financial services; and the blending of the security and communications industry have formed one of the most powerful tools to be used in the end- time theater to set the stage for the coming of Jesus Christ. These converged elements from a functional perspective will be used for two primary purposes—first, communications, and second, commerce.

Communications are critical to the success of creating a global community. We have witnessed in our lifetime the power of TV to influence society. It has been said that elections are won or lost on TV. The TV has shown us things in "real time" that make us feel as if we are part of the process. It has made our world seem a much smaller place. With the advent of news networks like CNN and their successful coverage of the Gulf War, we were placed in the midst of the battle theater from the comfort and safety of our living room.

TV has put us on the moon, under the ocean, in orbit around the earth, in the midst of starving world populations, at parties, in people's homes, in front of others' families, and their private lives. You name it, and TV has been there to make you feel a part of the action. Look at the recent craze of "Reality TV." This venue of TV programming seems to be growing in popularity. Now, you are placed in the actors' homes, bathrooms, and bedrooms and get to witness their activities—real time. Wow! How times have changed!

Advertising companies have learned the power of the TV to influence the sales of products and services and have created a bombardment of commercials designed to appeal to our emotions and sensuality. You cannot sit down in front of the TV, even in an airplane, and not have commercials blaring every 15 minutes unless you pay for such a service from the entertainment industry. Why? Because it works! Think about how much advertisers pay for 30-second time slots during events like the Super Bowl—millions of dollars. Advertising is so effective that advertising agencies even have awards, such as the Clio Awards, for the creation of the most effective commercials.

Studies have been done on TV's ability to influence its viewers to do violent acts. TV programs are filled with violent content in the name of "action television." These real-to-life acts of violence show people being beaten, shot, stabbed, kicked, punched, and blown up. You name it, and TV has maimed it. TV has helped diminish our value for human life. We have become de-sensitized to violence and death because of the hundreds of thousands of acts of violence we have seen over our lifetimes on TV, read in the newspapers, or viewed as part of the entertainment industry. It should be no surprise that children are killing other children and adults in our schools and people are crashing into buildings and killing thousands of innocent people. The perpetrators have seen it all on TV.

My daughter was in Mexico during the terrorist attack on the World Trade Center towers. She reported a sad reality to me that illustrates what we expect to see on TV and how reality and the entertainment industry have crossed over in our mind's eye. She said that one of the people she was with asked, as they watched the coverage of the planes crashing into the towers, "What movie is this from?" We have grown to expect to see such sensational destruction from filmmakers in action movies in the name of entertainment. The person had no idea that this was true "Reality TV" and that thousands of people had actually died in this violent and cruel act of terrorism.

Sexuality and sensuality are hot topics for TV today with more and more explicit content making its way even to network TV. The networks have recently said that to effectively compete with the cable industry, they must put more adult content on network TV. Otherwise they fear that they will not be able to keep their advertisers and viewing audiences. It is not uncommon to see sexual innuendo in teen programs as well as graphic content in programs targeted for adults. We now regularly see homosexual content on TV along with regular bombardments of adulterous affairs and relationships outside of marriage. Advertisers use sex to promote their products as a matter of course. We cannot hide ourselves from the influence of sexuality on the TV, unless we turn the TV off.

This is a notion, but unfortunately, it is not a trend that is happening worldwide. Rather TV viewing is on the rise. TV is part of our life, not being too far from us anywhere we might be conducting life's activities. Think about it. TVs are in offices, homes, stores, restaurants, cars, buses, planes, trains, and in portable form that we carry—everywhere.

We no longer gather around the radio for information. Rather we gather around the TV, and it is literally in our face. We are almost powerless to pull ourselves from it once we are in its grasp. I recall that with the 2001 attack on New York and Washington people, including myself, were glued to the TV set. I personally could not move from the news broadcasts whether on the TV or on my computer. I was keeping a mental note as to the power of this media, because I planned to soon write this chapter, and what timing! The media lived up to my expectation—the power of appealing to the eyes is an almost transcendental state.

TV is effective because it appeals to the "lust of the eyes." Mankind was deceived as a people (by Satan in the garden) based on sight ("Does it not look good for food?") as well as on pride and covetousness ("You will be like God, understanding good and evil.") It is easy to keep our attention if you show us something that we enjoy looking at or that impacts our life.

TV as a technology has been used by Satan, who is the prince of the power of the air. No wonder it has been so effective as it rides the airwaves, carrying its message and influence to society. In contrast, what Satan has intended to use for harm and for his purposes, God has used for good in the furtherance of the gospel message worldwide.

TV has been the most powerful technology tool used by evangelists around the world to present the gospel to all nations. I was told that the recent Billy Graham message, which was preached during the service in Washington, D.C., after the terrorist attack, was broadcast all over the world. This is sobering, when you consider that the Bible says that Jesus will not come until all the nations have come under the sound of the gospel message. I think we can say, at least logistically (via satellite broadcast over the airwaves), that the entire world has now "come under the broadcast airwaves" of the gospel message. Jesus could come at any time as a result of this fulfillment of scriptural prophecy. I know an argument exists, that not all people groups have been *physically reached*. I would ask you to consider, that this view is a matter of perspective. Technologies, beyond the comprehension of Biblical writers, have now, physically, blanketed the entire world with the "sound" of the gospel.

TV will continue to be a platform, which is important for communications during the end-time theater. New technologies that blend TV and the Internet have emerged, making it possible to get TV broadcasts right over the Internet on your computer, a palm top or Personal Digital Assistant (PDA), and even advanced mobile phones with color browser screens. Because of communication advances offering the needed "high bandwidth" or "big pipes" required for video, you can hardly tell the difference between the TV and the Internet via a computing device. This is the essence of convergence, which is taking place right now. It brings the benefits and acceptance of TV into computers and integrates the financial capabilities of Internet to create a visual access portal for e-commerce and global communications.

The blending of the Internet to TV is important for two reasons. The first reason is the furtherance of TV's reach to Internet-enabled computing devices that are becoming more and more mobile. This is important because the Antichrist will not want you far from a TV, because he will want you to see and hear his message and propaganda about world events. Also, the convergence is needed so that TV can benefit from the financial reach of the e-commerce network that is being offered via the Internet.

The phrase "seeing is believing" gives an idea as to the importance of sight relevant to our ability to align with or evaluate something's truth. The phrase "I can't believe my eyes," which would be expressed when a person undergoes shock as a result of what they have just seen or witnessed, gives you a clue of the power of sight to persuade—sight can even have you challenge your own intellect.

Jesus knew the power of sight to persuade the masses as He conducted his public ministry. People witnessed the healings of the blind, crippled, demon possessed, and lepers; the feeding of thousands from five loaves and two fish; and even the raising of the dead. Christ Himself rose from the dead and showed Himself to his disciples and the masses before His ascension to the Heavens. He had promised to go to prepare a place for us, Heaven, and then He promised to come back for us again so that we can be with Him and spend eternity with the Creator who loved us and gave Himself for us. In the Book of John Jesus said this to his disciples, and it applies to us today:

> "Do not let your hearts be troubled. Trust in God; trust also in me. In my Father's house are many rooms (or mansions in some translations);

if it were not so, I would have told you. I am going there to prepare a place for you. And if I go and prepare a place for you, I will come back and take you to be with me that you also may be where I am. You know the way to the place where I am going." Thomas said to him, "Lord, we don't know where you are going, so how can we know the way?" Jesus answered, "I am the way and the truth and the life. No one comes to the Father except through me. If you really knew me, you would know my Father as well. From now on, you do know him and have **seen him**." Philip said, "Lord, **show us** the Father and that will be enough for us." Jesus answered: "Don't you know me, Philip, even after I have been among you such a long time? Anyone who has **seen me** has **seen the Father**. How can you say, **"Show us the Father?"** Don't you believe that I am in the Father, and that the Father is in me? The words I say to you are not just my own. Rather, it is the Father, living in me, who is doing his work. Believe me when I say that I am in the Father and the Father is in me; or at least believe on the evidence of the miracles themselves." (John 14:1-11).[xi]

Philip's comments are so much like ours. Show us the Father, and that will be enough for us. We need to see it with our eyes. Jesus knows this and answers Philip, saying, "Anyone who has seen me has seen the Father." Yet He questions Philip, saying "Don't you know me after being with me this long?" Basically, "Can't you believe what you are seeing with your own eyes?" All of the miracles are evidence of His power, even His power over death. This feels like a living example of "I can't believe my eyes!"

Satan also knows the power of sight and desires to counterfeit the things of God. He understands the power of resurrection over death as exemplified by Christ's death and resurrection from the grave. During the end-times theater, the Book of Revelation says that the Antichrist will have a fatal wound of a sword that will be healed. One could assume that this could be a result of a catastrophic event such as an assassination. In this case, the people of the world, who will be following this great leader's actions of peace, will be mourning his death. Later, when he is raised from the dead, having "his fatal wound healed," he will begin to have deity-like qualities. We all wish for power over death and would likely follow after anyone who has had victory over death–especially if we "saw it with our own eyes."

Satan, who is controlling the actions of the Antichrist, will use the power of TV and the Internet to broadcast this counterfeit resurrection over the airwaves to turn the hearts of people to worship the Antichrist in awe of what they have "seen with their own eyes." This resurrection is counterfeit, because it is only a resurrection of the body and not of the soul. Only Jesus Christ can give eternal life to a person's soul. Jesus said, "I am the way, the truth, and the life. No man comes to the Father but by Me."

Visual media has been the most effective and farthest-reaching communication tool ever used to reach the masses and to create a global community. This will continue to be an important tool in the last days as our world, which is falling under the judgment of a holy God, seeks answers amidst the chaos. The answer continues to be Jesus Christ, but it is said that many will be deceived during this time, believing the lies of Satan and the Antichrist, because they have come in the name of good, peace, equality for mankind, tolerance and everything that appeals to the emotions and goodness of mankind. The Antichrist will be telling us what we want to hear during these trying times and using the visual media to accomplish this task.

The inevitable marriage between the TV and the computer (or the Internet) has been coming for a long time. It is natural to blend TV with the computer because they have commonality in how they reach their audience with sight, sound, and touch. You see, with your eyes on a screen, the TV or computer content resulting from your physical touch via controls on the TV, remote control, keyboard, or mouse, and you hear the audio played through speakers connected to the TV or computer.

The access method and outputs are very similar, and the full multimedia experience appeals to three of our five senses—sight, hearing, and touch. The very nature of the experience can virtually include the other two senses of smell and taste, because your mind has the ability to imagine and project past experiences of like nature to round out the visual experience—"It looks so good you can almost taste it." Another term for this is virtual reality.

Both technologies require large amounts of bandwidth or big pipes to broadcast the content. As a result, the Internet has been able to benefit from the existing infrastructure that exists to provide TV programming, helping it solve the speed or "response-time issues" it has for users just using a dial-up account through their local phone lines. Dial-up accounts are very slow, and because of the heavy graphics and multimedia content being placed on Internet sites today, dial-up accounts have become quite inadequate and nonfunctional for most e-commerce and video applications.

An example of leveraging TV infrastructure is "high-speed Internet access" or connectivity via the cable provider's coax or fiber cable, which runs into your home. You place a device on the cable (which currently provides your TV programming) to allow the cable to talk with your computer; the device is called a "cable modem." Modems are used as communication devices between computers to allow them to share information with each other.

Another example is Digital Subscriber line (DSL), which is generally provided by your local telephone company. This is similar in concept in that you have a DSL modem that allows your current telephone line coming into your home to be connected to your computer, providing you with high-speed access.

Yet one more connection model is wireless, and I believe it will soon be very prevalent because of its ease and speed of installation, as it no longer requires the expensive and time-consuming need to dig or hang physical infrastructure to reach the masses. This includes various technologies, such as microwave, mobile cellular, and satellite mediums for connectivity. We will discuss communications and their importance and implications in the next chapter.

Leverage of TV infrastructure, including fiber-optic and coaxial cable to the home, satellite and wireless technologies, and the creation of technologies to enhance the speed of slower mediums such as the telephone wires to your home (referred to as copper connections), is effectively providing the high-speed super highway needed for the future of e-commerce and a cashless society. This improved performance has become the impetus for even further use and benefit from the Internet and computer capabilities in your home. Now you can access business applications offered on line to provide you service on your bank accounts, make purchases for goods and services, conduct research, play games, gamble, buy lottery tickets, get mapping information, watch live TV broadcasts, or replay video events as presented on various web sites. It is making the craze of the Internet yet farther reaching. These touch points have been named many things, and I will list them just for sake of information. Examples are:

B2C (Business to Consumer), which is the marketing of goods and services to consumers by business that are on line. This includes financial services such as bank-at-home-type functions. This concept is also referred to as e-commerce.

B2B (Business to Business), which is the connection of businesses to one another so that they can benefit by savings that electronic networking can bring. The connections are used for purchasing parts to fulfill orders and for electronic payments. This has previously been known as EDI, and current Internet technologies are expanding the reach of this known concept. This concept is also referred to as e-manufacturing.

B2E (Business to Employee), which is the provision of all types of inter-company information via the Internet or what is called Intranet in this application, because it is inside the company, hidden from those outside because of the confidential nature of the information. This use of the Internet is generally called a "portal," and, like the name, it is an entry point to human resources (HR), knowledge repositories, on-line order entry systems, and customer relationship management systems (CRM). This is becoming very popular and saving employers millions of dollars from increased efficiencies and lower costs of operation.

The successful adoption and use of B2E portals will drive more advanced B2B interconnections and further the intertwining of businesses electronically so that they can remain more competitive in an increasingly more difficult world economy.

The craze of the Internet itself is worth a brief mention before we converge the financial elements into the total visual media story. Just reflect with me on the massive expansion of this technology and literally the craze that it has created in the business and financial communities. It might surprise you that the Internet, or at least its early beginnings started in the late 1950s with the formation of a group called ARPA (Advanced Research Projects Agency) whose purpose was to establish a U.S. lead for science and technology applicable to the military. In 1969, ARPANET was commissioned by the Department of Defense, and this was the start of the Internet as we know it today. I will not go through a detailed history of the Internet, because this is available on line by simply doing a search for "history of the Internet" (put this in a search engine with quotes just as it is typed above). Doing this search will result in "a ton" of information available for you to read. Some key highlights start in 1991 with the birth of the

World Wide Web (www), which is currently used today to reach Internet sites worldwide.

From 1991 through 1995, agencies such as the World Bank, the United Nations, and the United States government went on line with sites. Things are starting to build and the explosion of the Internet, which has turned twenty-five years old in 1994, is just about to become the craze of the 21st century.

In 1995, companies such as CompuServe, America Online (AOL) and Prodigy came on the scene to provide public dial-up access to the Internet, using standard telephone lines and modems, then at speeds of 9600 bits per second (BPS). In laymen's terms this speed was "dog slow" but was nothing short of a miracle, because now you could communicate with a friend across the country or around the world using a new tool and communications phenomenon called e-mail. AOL made it famous with its automated message notification phrase that says, "You've Got Mail." Tom Hanks and Meg Ryan starred in a romantic comedy using that phrase for a title and featuring the famous AOL trademark. The couple met on line through AOL and started to correspond. Eventually they physically met because of a string of circumstances revolving around common business endeavors. The movie leaves you with the idea that these two will live happily ever after.

From 1996 to the present, the Internet has become a craze for businesses and, for all intents and purposes, is analogous to a feeding frenzy. The notion that companies could be on line and connect to markets around the world to sell their products and services, thereby extending their reach to farther-than-imaginable places with current technology and business practices, drove strategists crazy. The fear of loss of these now-global markets because of the creation of this electronic community was bringing out the best of our greed nature, even to the point of making "stupid business decisions." Investors started to pump billions of dollars into companies that simply had ideas of how they could leverage the Internet to sell products and services.

This gave rise to the dot.com era (renamed the dot.bomb era in 2001), which was typically characterized by the twenty-something entrepreneur who was computer savvy and understood how to spell World Wide Web and could figure out how to program in HTTP (an Internet programming language) and could talk TCP/IP, the Internet networking protocol (or language) that connects the machines together. Most of them lacked in business knowledge or experience, but that wasn't necessary, because investors were willing to give away billions of dollars to be part of the game. Having been a self-employed in small business for 17 years of my 20+ years in the industry, I can tell you that it is no wonder that things "fell in the toilet." Companies were left to run amuck spending money on ridiculous things—thousands of dollars on office furniture, buildings, massive computer systems, and employee salaries that were going through the roof because of supply and demand issues, and on and on.

Investors and these new dot.bombers forgot one basic principal of business 101—"you must create in your business endeavor more revenue than you spend!" It's a basic concept, I know, but you can look at the market today and realize that no one was giving this principal too much consideration. As my wife would say, "They were all betting on the come," or, in other words, speculating for the future financial win. So why did this take place and was it for naught? I say no! This needed to take place to set the stage for the adoption of further implementations of the cashless society. This craze made the entire world conscious of being connected together to do business and create community. Without such hype, it could have taken years to get to where we are today. After all, the Internet had already been in existence for 25 years. Why, all of a sudden, did the world get so excited? It's time!

The infrastructure is now in place to conduct business around the world, and with this new capability, it is driving more advanced methods or transacting business electronically (see the previous financial and security chapters). As a result, and particularly of late, the investment market is now focusing on revenue and profits to come out of this stock market dot.bomb slump. Businesses will now need to make all this craziness work to create revenue and profit (Business 101) so that they can continue to receive capital from the investment communities. As a result, they will be looking for easier and more standard ways to leverage the global infrastructure. Adherence to open standards to create Internet programs, security models, financial models, and any other developing technologies that can assure fast success and quick time to market with offered products and services will be high on the priority list of companies.

So, in the end, it comes down to simple motivations—the fear of loss (pain) created a rush by investors to give money to people so that they wouldn't miss the train pulling out. Businesses were motivated by pleasure (getting money to build their dream and live high on the hog) to produce infrastructure, ideas, working products, and not-so-working products. Now businesses, based on market conditions, are faced with pain as a motivation to get their act together and get profitable or no more investment capital. The investors are now waiting to have their relief from the pain of bad investments and get a little pleasure by the end payoff of global expanding markets and a functional, cashless electronic society. I am sure that at the end of the day, they will get theirs, too.

This is all a large intertwined cycle interconnecting many industries (we will discuss these relationships in the chapter on e-commerce), but it ultimately comes back to one simple thing—"the money."

The money is what we will now focus on, relevant to the convergence of the TV and the computer or the Internet. This convergence of making the Internet accessible via the TV has created a new "access portal" to conduct business electronically and will continue to be an important part of the end-time theater, as we are very comfortable with the TV, and its reach is global.

Convergence of Industries—Content Providers, Merchants, and Financial Institutions

Various industries will financially benefit from the convergence of the TV and the Internet or the computer. The blending of broadcast TV with the Internet is expanding the reach of the broadcast and entertainment industries, as well as the financial community, into the homes of anyone who has a TV. The result of this convergence is the creation of a new access portal that will provide consumers with a media-rich experience to receive broadcast and entertainment content and to make electronic purchases, leveraging the global marketplace and popularity of the Internet.

The players, including broadcast stations, entertainment conglomerations, computer companies, financial institutions, and communications companies (cable and telecom industries), are trying to gain control of the monetary benefits associated with providing consumers with the set top box and needed software and services required to provide easy access to the global electronic network to purchase goods and services and receive content from the comfort, convenience, and safety of your own home.

The set top box is the device that connects your TV to the TV broadcasting network and the Internet to allow access to e-mail, World Wide Web, your on-line banking accounts, merchants, and any and all of your entertainment content, which, by the way, you can order on demand when you want it. The set top box is also responsible for converting digital signal transmissions to analog transmission so that your current analog TV set can display the digital information on the screen. In effect, the set top box turns your TV monitor into a digital computer that can be used for your entertainment, to conduct business electronically, and to provide you with information about things happening in your neighborhood or around the world.

The limit of computing possibilities will be tied directly to your set top box—the more advanced, the more features. This will be a primary growth area, as this sector of the technology industry has very few globally accepted standards at this time. New laws, which we will discuss later in this chapter, are scheduled to make analog broadcasting obsolete in 2006, mandating that all TV transmission be digital in nature. I suspect that this will become a business driver for the industry to get its act together. The challenge is that financially, much can be gained or lost at this junction, so the stakes are high, and organizations are moving cautiously. One bad move, and a player could be out of the game, a powerful and profitable game, forever!

The uniqueness and power of a TV "access portal" are that it is familiar and less intimidating than the computer. You will simply be able to use your remote control, or voice commands (in the future) while sitting in front of your TV, which the average person does for more than four hours a day, and order your favorite TV program, a pizza, or that special birthday gift; send an e-mail to Mom, and pay for it securely with your new Smart Card without ever getting out of your favorite chair! Oh, I forgot, you would need to get up to answer the door to get the pizza so that you could eat and enjoy your dinner. I guess some things can't be replaced by technology, at least for now!

This may sound facetious, but it is true: Players in this new virtual global electronic society are working to leverage every marketing channel possible to obtain your customer loyalty. The blending of TV with the Internet is an important frontier because it leverages a familiar, accepted, and broadly used technology, TV with the computer, which is used to access electronic systems worldwide via the Internet. Many people around the world have purchased PCs for their home to access the Internet, but it has not reached the same saturation as that of the television set.

The word "frontier" is a true reflection of the condition of the broadcast industry or the TV networks. Changes are being mandated by such agencies as the Federal Communications Commission (FCC), requiring the TV networks responsible for broadcasting TV programming to convert their systems to a digital signal transmission from that of the current analog model, which has been prevalent since the invention of TV. This schedule requires that stations affiliated with the top four networks (ABC, CBS, FOX, and NBC) in the 10 largest markets must have begun service by May 1, 1999. Stations affiliated with these networks in markets 11-30 must have begun service by November 1, 1999. All commercial stations must have begun digital TV (DTV) service by May 1, 2002, and all noncommercial educational stations must have started DTV service by May 1, 2003. Stations were allowed two 6-month extensions just by filing a request. The full FCC must grant any additional extensions after appropriate review of the request from a noncompliant broadcasting station. The plan is, that during the next few years, starting in April 2003, 50% of the analog programming will be simulcast on one of the DTV channel programs, 75% by April 2004, and 100% by April 2005. In theory, analog TV can be turned off in 2006, but that depends on how many people still rely on their analog TVs, which can get DTV via the set top box.

In the United States, broadcast providers are complaining about this conversion to digital transmission because of the loss of channels from the amount of bandwidth the digital transmission requires for high-definition TV (HDTV) programming. It is said that one HDTV broadcast could carry six analog channels in the same space. For service providers or networks that are concerned about the sales of advertising space during program broadcasting, the loss of channels could be significant.

In addition, the United States markets are caught up with the amount of channels we have available not that 100 plus channels aren't enough, but movement to this new digital transmission model could cut down on the number of channels that could be selected. Now we might have only 50 channels to scan before we find out that there is nothing on worth watching.

In other areas around the world, such as Europe, the Middle East, and China, companies like Nokia are finding inroads providing a set top box that is now being called a "multimedia home terminal." The set top box will provide access to digitally broadcasted network programming and will provide Internet access for converged communications. Adoption of HDTV seems better in these parts of the world. The British surveyed (64%) said that they are not in need of more than 25 channels of high-quality programming and that 67% would prefer to get their quality programming through a standard aerial antenna versus a satellite dish.[xii] China will also benefit, as an early adopter, from the rollout of HDTV as a primary way to extend the Internet to the home for access to advanced broadcasting services.[xiii]

So again it seems, that in other parts of the world, there are developments of advanced technologies that are being embraced by countries that have defined roles in the end-time theater without the adoption of such technology by the United States markets. HDTV and Smart Cards are two such technologies that are much more successful in other parts of the world than in the United States. It always raises a question in my mind as to where and what the Americas do during the end-time theater—the Bible is not clear on this subject.

So what does all this digital stuff mean, and what does it practically provide in the big scheme of things? Digital transmission of TV signals makes TV broadcasts more like computers and computer networking (remember the Internet is a computer network), which uses digital signals for transmission. I will not belabor this, but as a practical point, it will make the integration of these two technologies simpler in the future because of no need for translations or conversions between the signaling formats (digital to analog and analog to digital). Fewer translations means less complexity, less cost, more efficiency, more security, and more leverage of standardization occurring in the computer industry.

This is a very complex subject, and my research has indicated that there are technical, political, and financial implications with this entire migration, at least in the United States. It will be an area that we can watch develop over time, particularly in countries around the world that will embrace this sooner than later. I am not sure that all of the programming hype of HDTV is the driver for this conversion. It is, of course, if you are selling technology or you are a quality critic needing the latest and greatest gizmo. I do, however, think that it has something to do with the importance of the world being on a common digital network for all types of communications and financial transactions. Digital networks for the TV and computers will be able to ubiquitously benefit from newly developed security methods and practices, as well as from chip-based financial technology discussed in previous chapters.

In the near future I expect more offerings like WebTV or whatever name your local network, cable operator, or satellite provider calls Internet access via the television in your area of the world. This service will blend TV programming, whether HDTV or standard broadcasts, with access to the Internet for surfing, e-mail, and on-line banking. This is an import access portal that needs to be developed so that people without computers in their home can have computer-like functions, via the set top box to do on-line banking or shopping via the Internet. Just think, from the comfort of your home, with your trusty remote control in your hand, you can purchase goods and services or even use your TV as a virtual ATM to put cash on your Smart Card so that you can have money for a cab ride or the vending machine or give someone cash on the way to school or work.

So what do we have at the end of the day? All of this technological mumbo jumbo will simply prove to be yet another infrastructure to connect a popular communication device, the TV, to the electronic global network, which will be used for communications and to financially conduct business in a cashless, electronic digital society.

I would love to tell you definitively as to how or when this may happen, but there are numerous scenarios based on areas of the world and technology. I will, however, leave you with this. It is not a question of when this convergence will take place, but rather a question of where and to what degree users will be able to leverage these concepts. Certainly it will be used in many places around the world to extend the reach of the Internet by providing wireless access via the broadcast airwaves. Additionally, it will provide access to Internet-based financial portals for purchases and electronic cash management for the new chip-based banking model. Now you are no further from an ATM machine then a walk to your nearest TV set. Now isn't that convenient?

You might say that the visual media, and practically, the Internet, have revolutionized the world, creating a global society that can conduct business worldwide electronically without cash, breaking down physical boundaries of time and space and issues of currency exchange. The visual media and the Internet have even bridged political and cultural barriers in the name of progress and commerce. It is truly a unique time in the history of mankind!

Dependencies and Holdouts

Visual media have a number of dependencies and holdouts that will affect the mass deployment of these various technologies and the applications, which will benefit from the deployment of this infrastructure. Keep in mind that they will converge, based on infrastructure availability and will likely do so at different times around the world based on such factors as market acceptance. We will focus first on TV broadcasting and then on Internet or computer issues.

Television Conversion to Digital Transmission

This is a complicated discussion, as you might have determined from reading this chapter. There are numerous issues that impact the deployment of digital transmission or HDTV, particularly in the United States. First, there are very few adopted standards that are being used by the constituents of this industry. There is a lot of infighting, merging, and jockeying for control of the content. The issue of the number of available channels versus the bandwidth of the broadcast frequency spectrum creates a revenue issue for advertising sales. Equipment is expensive and is being mandated by the government.

There is paradigm shift from information being controlled by the networks and the producers to information being controlled by the consumer. This raises yet more complex business questions relevant to controlling viewing times and ratings. This type of control by the networks has allowed them to ascertain statistics about viewer habits and sell slots of time for advertising based on demographics information, which could create a supply and demand value proposition for pricing their advertising services. The best example is a major sporting event with a large following. This type of slot could literally cost millions of dollars for a 30-second commercial. With the consumer in control, leveraging digital technology, everything, as we know it today, would change. This creates a fear for some companies—hence the resistance to change.

I think the notion of the computer merging with broadcast TV also removes some of the control and mystique, as there will be computer standards that can and will be leveraged to provide broadcast content over the Internet to all types of devices, especially those that are wireless in nature. Basically, if you are a network and are not streaming content and creating revenue by sending information or programming to both the TV and

Internet, you're probably missing the boat. This is why mega mergers like America Online and Time Warner, Inc., are taking place and being watched so closely—it is the blending of content delivery and Internet connectivity in a massive, almost monopolistic-like way. I think you will see more of these types of mergers in the future as organizations realize the inevitable: television's content delivery and the entertainment industry are going to converge with the Internet to create a feature-rich interactive environment that puts the world at the fingertips of the consumer.

Internet Readiness for Convergence

The Internet, at this time, only lacks a few major things to continue its transformation of the world into an electronic global marketplace. The first thing it lacks is a communications issue called "the last mile." The last mile is the connection from an Internet service provider who can provide an adequate high-speed connection, which can handle the graphic contents now displayed on web sites. This can be done with any communications medium that can do the job (we will be discussing this in the next chapter). The second thing the Internet lacks is the continued adoption and use of advanced security models (discussed in the last chapter) to assure a person's identity and protect his or her electronic currency.

The last mile is currently a major holdout because of the current capabilities of terrestrial strategies including coaxial cable, fiber-optic cable, and copper cable that must be physically installed. The need for Internet connectivity because of its global popularity and place in end-time history cannot further wait on the time it takes to physically install this type of connection to your home or place of business. In addition to time constraints, it is very costly and labor intensive to physically install this type of infrastructure, particularly in places around the world that are less developed and require trenching or poles to be placed to get services out to the populace for distribution.

Current Internet Service Providers (ISPs) with infrastructure are also limiting the mass adoption of high-speed connectivity because of high monthly charges billed to consumers for the service. This current pricing model is based on limited competition between other terrestrial ISPs offering similar services. Until the wireless market truly matures, this will not change, because the ISPs (mainly telecomm and cable companies) are trying squeeze out their last bit of return on investment for physical assets that are in the ground before these assets become of less value because of wireless vendors building networks around them and eroding away their customer base by offering faster, more cost-effective connectivity.

Wireless technology will become a driving force in the global expansion of the Internet and will provide the solution to the last mile dilemma. This technology will include satellite, advanced digital cellular, and various other models. Some methods require equipment placed on the ground to send out signals, which can be received with or without a direct line of site to the physical location, depending on the technology, or satellite, which simply needs a small dish pointed to the sky in the appropriate direction. I am sure that in the future, the direction of the dish will become less relevant, because satellites can now blanket areas with signals for such applications as radio programming. HDTV will also be able to provide wireless Internet connectivity as this is rolled out to various areas around the world, leveraging digital broadcasting technology to separate TV broadcast programming from the Internet, yet converging them for a more media-rich experience using an advanced set top box or multimedia home terminal.

Another holdout is the development and distribution of set top boxes. Manufacturers will need to create these products in such a way that makes them (the set top box or Multimedia Home Terminal) able to generically connect to whatever type of medium is available (cable, fiber, copper, or satellite), while providing the needed computing and broadcasting functionality to fully leverage the global electronic network. The set top box or Multimedia Home Terminal will also need to support Smart Card standards that have been adopted by the financial community so that consumers can securely make purchases over the Internet and use the box as a virtual ATM machine for electronic currency management.

Standards compliance for Smart Cards will not be a problem, because most of these boxes already use Smart Cards for access control. Just pull out your little card, and you will see some contacts on the card that transmit information from the microchip that is contained on the card to the set top box. A microchip may already be in use in your home, and you didn't even know it, or maybe you did know and didn't care, because it brought you wonderful TV programming on demand. See how easily it sneaks into our lives.

Distribution of the set top boxes could also be a holdout for mass distribution to consumers because of the expense of the appliance. To leverage the vast potential of the TV's impact on the world, this will need to be a global distribution. I think that you will initially see these products being sold to consumers for advanced feature functionality such as digital recording of TV broadcasts. Set top boxes could potentially replace the Video Cassette Recorder (VCR) as a recording device because of the quality of the recorded image and the convenience of use. But additional features will not put this in every home that has a TV set around the world. What will put this in every home is a free offer from someone who stands to benefit financially by making the technology available to you. If it can make your life a little easier or safer, you might let them give you such as gizmo. It feels a little like a toaster.

There are a number of candidates to make such an offer happen, and there is successful financial precedence for creating a business case to make such an offer. The cable and satellite providers have been providing set top boxes for years to control your access to TV programming offered by their company. They gain a monthly reoccurring fee and pay-per-view fees for such a device and have a rate of return that can be projected, based on past history, to drive the replacement of their current boxes to these new advanced systems. This upgrade will also create new sources of revenue from the same customer because of additional features and services available when using the new appliance.

Financial institutions could also have an interest in providing such a device to their customers. In the early years of electronic banking, there was resistance to deploying ATMs because of the expense and the paradigm change it represented to the banking industry. Banks have since learned that these 24-hour-a-day workhorses never eat, don't complain, rarely take breaks, and provide customers with service equal to or better than a human teller. ATMs have also proved to be a source of recurring revenue because customers are now charged transaction fees for using ATMs.

Financial institutions understand the value of making a few cents on each transaction and how much pennies can represent, when you consider the millions of transactions processed each day.

Advanced chip-based electronic banking models could greatly benefit by such a device, making it easy for banking customers like you to conduct banking business with your Smart Card and make secured purchases using this new access portal—the TV conveniently located right in your own home. I don't think it will be very hard to sell senior banking executives, this time around, on the idea of providing their customers with a virtual ATM machine that is located in their living room. The math should speak for itself! Keep your eye on this group, as financial institutions have much to gain. Such offers could also come in the form of partnerships with other service providers, broadcasting companies, or entertainment companies.

Technology companies (computer and software vendors) are also trying to get in the game. Organizations that support connectivity to the Internet with hardware or software are trying to figure out ways to capture and bill for transactions over the Internet. Microsoft is the best example. Microsoft provides Internet connectivity and services via Microsoft Network (MSN), is involved in the broadcasting industry as exemplified by MSNBC on TV and via the Internet, and its set top box offering WebTV, which is working on doing all that we have discussed in this chapter. Microsoft is also participating heavily in the security marketplace with its Passport product for secured transaction processing over the Internet. With its fingers in so many pots, some might think that Microsoft has a little monopoly going. Many of these companies are connected with a variety of income sources associated with e-commerce. The players to watch who may make this move are those who are invested in many other service areas that could benefit by providing access to Internet via a TV access portal. Companies such as Microsoft, IBM, SUN, HP, Oracle, Sony, Nokia—basically, the giants in the industry, could all have motives for investing in such a device as long as they could connect to a reoccurring revenue stream.

The previously mentioned names, other than Microsoft, are just for discussion. I have not researched if they have specific interest in this space. They just all possess the commonality of industry involvement and the financial strength to engage in such an initiative. I believe that Microsoft, however, is targeting this space and will play a role in converging the TV and computer into a usable interactive access portal to leverage this global electronic communications and financial network called the Internet.

I could discuss additional factors such as software standardization, but the focus of this chapter is on the blending of these two areas of technology to create a converged media-rich experience for watching TV broadcasts, gaming, shopping, communicating (by e-mail, phone calling, and video conferencing), and banking, all from a visual access portal located in your home or business. My hope is that you will watch (see with your own eyes) and be conscious of the emergence of these things in your neighborhood and living room, and with such an awareness, know that Jesus Christ is coming again, and sooner with each passing day. Are you ready to meet Him, or will He surprise you like a thief in the night?

In closing, visual media will continue to be a key ingredient in e-commerce and global communications. For the most part visual media are completely functional. The holdouts we have discussed just enhance the reach and functionality of these media. They are fully functional today to control the buying and selling of goods and services, based on current levels of technology adaptation and functionality. New capabilities will just be layered on as global events continue to drive us like sheep to the acceptance and use of more advanced technologies that will provide us with greater levels of function, safety, and convenience, all from of our favorite chair, sitting in front of our old friend, the TV, or our new friend, the wireless pocket computer, anywhere, anytime our little heart desires. Now isn't that special! After all, this is all about you. Or is it?

Notes:

[xi] Bold text was added by the author for emphasis.
[xii] Nokia press release dated September 24, 1998. The representative sample was of 1008 adults, age 15 or above.
[xiii] Nokia press release dated November 30, 2000, regarding strategic relationship with Sichuan NTC Investment Co., Ltd.

Chapter Five

The Communications Industry

The Evolution of Communications

In this last and final technology section, we will review the evolution of the communications industries relevant to e-commerce and the development of a cashless society. Communications infrastructure is a critical component to an electronic society because it is responsible for interconnecting all of the computing devices together so that they can share information and provide services of all types to users on the network. In regard to the mass deployment of a global electronic communications and commerce infrastructure, communication's most visible role to users is that of the "last mile" connection.

The term "last mile" represents the final connection into the home or place of business that provides the subscriber of a telephone, TV or data service with the needed connection to the desired "carrier" or "provider" of the service. For example, if you have a telephone, the wire that comes into your home that connects your telephone to the nearest "central office (CO) is your last mile connection. If you subscribe to cable TV, the cable that runs from an "underground pedestal" near or in your back yard or from a pole near your home via a drop cable is your last mile connection for TV programming. In like manner, the method you use to connect to your

ISP for Internet connectivity to surf the web, access financial services, purchase merchandise, or ascertain information, is considered your last mile connection.

The Internet, because of the design architecture and nature of the service, has many last mile options, including dial-up via a telephone line, cable modem, DSL, satellite, advanced cellular networks, or other wireless models. The option you choose is generally driven by the physical choices that are available in your area and the type of speed you need when using the Internet. We will discuss this in more detail later in the chapter, as it is key to the global expansion of the Internet and is currently the technical holdout for mass global expansion.

For the sake of background (so that you can understand how we got here and why we are currently unable to meet the growing demand of Internet last mile connectivity), I will share a brief evolution of the industry. As I have said before, this is not designed to be a comprehensive look at this specific industry, because this subject alone could comprise the total contents of a book. Simply go to amazon.com, and I am sure you will find many reference books available if you have further interest in this subject. I just want to lay the groundwork so that you can see that there are technical, political, and financial constraints impacting current methods of last mile expansion as they relate to terrestrial-type connectivity—

connections made with physical media of any type such as copper, coaxial, or fiber-optic cables.

Telecommunications—A Brief History

The communications industry began with the invention of the telephone by Alexander Graham Bell. This led to the early name of the first communications monopoly in the United States, "The Bell System," which was later more compassionately nicknamed "Ma Bell." The official name was American Telephone and Telegraph Company (AT&T).

With the invention of the telephone, communications would never be the same. The telephone soon replaced the telegraph, which used Morse code to tap out the message, with the pleasant, simpler sound of a voice coming out of a little box on a wall or a desk. The concept took off like wildfire and expanded across the United States by the stringing of copper wires from place to place. The wires were interconnected through switches (i.e., central office switches) so that people could eventually dial one another without operator assistance. "It was the next best thing to being there." Well, this phase came later in history, with the promotion of making frequent long-distance calls because of the low cost in comparison to traveling to see loved ones or friends. The phone changed our lives and made our world seem to be a smaller place. Now in a matter of seconds, you could be connected to loved ones or business associates across the street, across the country, or around the world.

Control of this powerful communications technology in the United States was in the hands of one company, AT&T, and it created a communications monopoly that would later be broken up in the late 1980s by a ruling by Judge Green from the Supreme Court. Around the world, countries, governments, and other independent organizations were expanding in like manner, endeavoring to control this powerful tool that would prove to be in the information era what rails were in the industrial era. Fortunes were made with these electronic highways that forged their way across the country and eventually the world to interconnect our societies so that they could communicate and conduct business globally.

It was perceived, and hence the motive for the breakup, that the control of such an asset by one company, or few companies around the world, was slowing the global expansion of the systems capabilities because of the lack of competition and consequent high prices for long-distance and local service costs. As a result, AT&T was broken up into pieces including local, long-distance, and equipment business ventures. AT&T retained the long-distance business and equipment manufacturing and sales. The Bell system, which was responsible for local service, was broken up into regional Bell operating companies (RBOCs). The RBOCs were not able to provide long-distance services outside their calling areas—for us in the telephone business, the terms were intra-LATA and inter-LATA calling. It was a confusing mess with the local RBOCs gouging callers for in-state calls and competitive long-distance carriers offering a way to bypass RBOC control through the use of a Primary Inter-LATA Code (PIC). A PIC allows callers to dial around the RBOC's network, resulting in a lower cost per minute for the same in-state call. Now when I say gouge, I mean it. Some in-state calls would cost 48 cents a minute via the RBOC versus a national call for 16 cents via a competitive carrier. In like manner, AT&T could not provide any type of local service or dial tone to the home or business, but AT&T was able to provide dedicated telecommunications for long-distance and computer network connectivity. This would later become an important business for AT&T as the world became more interconnected with computing devices. The telephone (communications) business was a lucrative game with fortunes made over the years. AT&T was a super power, and this is why AT&T fought so hard to avoid having the system taken apart. Monopoly is a great game if you control all the spaces on the board.

The breakup made way for long-distance companies to compete for your long-distance dollars. AT&T and the RBOCs had to provide what was called "equal access" to companies like Sprint, MCI, and other emerging-long distance carriers so that you could dial 1 plus a number, just like you did with AT&T. Prior to this time you needed to dial an 800 number and authorization code from your long-distance company or a seven digit PIC code to bypass AT&T's service to place a long-distance call on an alternative carrier's network. This made calling cumbersome and unequal, hence the need for a change.

Judge Green's rulings and provisions of the breakup mandated this equal access for long distance and later even equal access to RBOCs so that competitive companies could offer alternatives for local services (dial tone) to your home or business, creating a more competitive environment. These companies were called Competitive Local Exchange Carriers (CLECs). The premise is that they would be granted rights to use the copper cable that comes into your home or business to interconnect to their equipment, which would be "co-located" in RBOC central office switching stations, so that you could complete a local call on their alternative service at a lower cost.

This breakup has been under way for years, and obviously, long-distance calling has successfully been made competitive. Expansion has taken place all over the world with an international call originating in the United States costing not much more than a call across the United States. It costs me about $0.12 to call Europe, in comparison to a cost of $2.00 or more per minute not long ago without such competition. A long-distance call across America is only $0.03-$0.04 per minute if you are a high volume user who has a discount plan with one of the carriers.

There has also been a paradigm change in the type of traffic that is traversing the communications networks. For the first time in history, data traffic (that being used for computing communications) is now exceeding voice communications. As a result of the globalization of society with the Internet, a new emphasis is being placed on capturing a company's computer networking connectivity. Soon, because of the rapidly falling cost per minute on voice calling, you will see voice services being offered for a flat-rate cost or free if the subscribing company gives the carrier all of their data business.

I could spend a lot of time discussing the political and financial implications of all this, but that is not what this book is about. Rather, let us focus on the issue at hand, which is last mile connectivity, because all of the evolution discussed above plays into the last mile dilemma. As I mentioned earlier in the chapter, last mile is the final connection that comes into your home or place of business and connects you to the carrier for voice services or an ISP to connect you to the Internet.

The rapid global expansion of the Internet and its need for more bandwidth than a telephone call has created a challenge for terrestrial carriers offering service to the masses. So that you have some technical background to understand these challenges, let us consider a few things. First, most of the communications networks that were built worldwide were created to carry voice traffic, which required a dedicated 64k path to be connected from one point to another. This path would be connected via a mesh of central office switches that were interconnected, and the path would remain connected until the parties "hung up" or disconnected. At that time, the switches disconnected the wires from the equipment needed to complete the call, and the systems would become available to place additional calls. Because most voice calls were short, the equipment could be engineered in such a way that many people could share the equipment in local areas and it would appear to them that they had dedicated resources, because whenever they wanted to make a call, they picked up the phone and dialed, and the equipment would complete the call if the party on the other end was able to answer the phone.

In contrast, the Internet is different in many respects. It is packet-based routed communications, which means that your computer interconnects to a mesh of boxes called routers. These routers know where other routers and destinations are on the worldwide network. The Internet uses naming conventions controlled by "Domain Name Servers," which are responsible for translating the name you type into the browser and mapping it to the IP address of the host server and application you require. The routers use the IP address to pick the shortest path to get your request processed. The IP address is like a phone number, unique to a computer or host computer and application that you are trying to reach. The nature of Internet communications is different from that of a voice call. Internet communications are longer, with average times on line of hours instead of minutes. As a result, of this shift in call duration, traditional telephone networks, which provide last mile access to the Internet via what is called dial-up service, have become overburdened with Internet traffic. In addition, the graphical content found on the Internet, that visually conveys a message, requires more bandwidth than today's 56k modems can adequately handle. Just as a note, modems started out at 9.6k for the Internet and now are 56k after say 6-8 years. This leveraged most of the 64k bandwidth available via a standard telephone line in your home. Modem manufacturers have tried every trick in the book, including advanced compression techniques, to increase the perceived speed of the modem, but the bottom line is that times are changing and we need more speed! "Scotty, I need more power." "Captain, I'm giving it all shees got!"

The telephone companies, or Regional Bell Operating Company (RBOC), have been trying to "give it all shees got," but they are in a bad situation. I believe that they, along with any carrier of any sort that relies solely on wired technology, is a modern-day dinosaur just waiting out a slow and eventual death. Telephone companies are particularly in a bad place, because their primary asset is copper in the ground and their switching stations. Because of de-regulations, they now have to share their central offices with Competitive Local Exchange Carriers (CLEC) who are competing with the same equipment, their equipment, at lower prices, which is cutting into their revenues. They continue having traffic problems, because customers are still using dial-up Internet accounts that tie up the central office equipment, making it unavailable for others to use for telephone calling. This creates regulatory service compliance issues, and RBOCs are getting fined for their inability to maintain required service levels to consumers. The only remedy for this is to spend more money to improve their networks, money that is scarce today.

Improving their networks is also a kiss of death, because as it breathes life into one area—reduced traffic on central offices and higher speed access to customers via DSL-type service offering, it kills their dedicated-line business for computer connections to business computers, which has been very lucrative in the past. I believe that is this business dilemma that has created an artificially slow rollout of high-speed services by RBOCs. For example, if you have a T-1 line (I know some of these terms are like Greek to some of you, but forgive me there is no other way to describe these things) dedicated to connect to the Internet for access to their ISP, it would cost about $800.00-$1,400.00 per month for the service from the RBOC. The speed is approximately 1.5 mbps, in comparison to a DSL line that might cost $100.00

for 1 mbps. Can you see the business problem? Why keep your dedicated T-1 at 10 times the monthly cost if you can have a DSL line put in instead and enjoy the savings? Well, this is the problem. If the RBOCs' mass-deploy DSL service to leverage their copper to give customers high-speed Internet access, which is what the customers want, then the RBOCs cut their own throats. As a result, you have witnessed a very slow rollout of these services around the country. The RBOCs are also faced with physical constraints of the technology because the DSL modems today have a limit of 20k kilo feet from the central office. The investment community also knows this fact, and there isn't enough money out there to rebuild and save the RBOCs from this plight unless they get creative with their wireless business. Hold that thought, because we have a little more to discuss about terrestrial communications.

Cable television companies are also providing last mile connections. The physical asset they have available (coax cable and fiber-optic cable) is more suited to the Internet, because it has more bandwidth and can provide customers with greater speeds. As a result, cable companies have been able to offer Internet connectivity with the addition of a cable modem, which acts like a small router, in your home to let one or many of your computers be on line at all times. What a concept—all the high-speed Internet you can "eat" for $39.00–$79.00 per month. So they solved the problem right. Well, not really, because they still have one common problem faced by all of the terrestrial carriers using physical medium for transport, and that is reach. If you do not have physical connectivity to an area, then you cannot provide service to that area. In addition, you have to add new equipment to your underground asset to make it usable by the Internet, and this takes time and money—money that is getting scarcer because of competition that is eroding the revenue base from lost subscribers or services.

I am an example of this, experiencing it firsthand in my life as I watched AT&T cable workers dig up my easement, smash down my grass, and do what they do when they are building out infrastructure. Yet when I called to check about availability, I got my favorite answer—"Sir, I'm sorry. @Home service isn't available in your area yet." Of course, my comment was, "Well, I suspect it should be anytime because I am looking out my window, and my yard is dug up, and they just installed fiber. Do you have any kind of dates or do you know the status of the build out?" The representative didn't know, but I later found out, after more calling and begging for information, that the fiber was in place, but the electronic equipment needed to connect me to the "mother ship" was not installed. I watched and waited for 2 years, and I still do not have Internet access via AT&T's cable available in my area. Fortunately, I used the same "regular badgering techniques" for the local wireless ISPs, and I finally got a 1-mbps dedicated connection in 2001 for $79.00 per month. Competition, established during the last four years, has since reduced this same service to $45.00 per month.

Now I am living proof of the loss of revenues being taken away from the cable companies, because of the lack of last mile facilities to extend their Internet service offerings. My wireless carrier, a regional ISP in the Rocky Mountain area, is also planning to encroach on the cable industry by expanding the bandwidth provided to me and in the future offering video on demand type programming. This is similar to cable and satellite TV's "pay per view." So, watch out, AT&T cable, because "wireless is yet again knocking on your door." As for me and my house, let the radio waves fry my brain, because I am ready to be done with the terrestrial providers last mile excuses!

The speed of growth of the Internet and the need to expand globally to reach more populace so that the stage can be set for end-time events can no longer afford the time it takes to install underground or overhead cables needed to connect a hungry world to this global electronic network. As a result, the wireless industry has emerged, and it is currently building infrastructure around these existing terrestrial networks to solve the last mile dilemma and provide global anytime, anywhere access to the network. Wireless is not new technology. We have been using it for years to communicate with TVs, radios, telephones, and microwaves (not the type you cook in, but microwave circuits for voice and data transmission). But this craze for global connectivity has given rise to new, advanced methods of wireless communications that are being deployed as we speak to provide us with more mobility, greater bandwidth, and converged features such as location (GPS), which is adding intelligence to mobile commerce (m-commerce) business applications.

Wireless technologies are advancing on a number of fronts, addressing various needs of Internet connectivity for home and business. The Internet functions as a Wide Area Network (WAN). It just so happens that its area is the world, so as we look at these technologies, they address various needs in the community for connectivity. For example, development is advancing in laser, microwave, and spread spectrum technologies to provide wireless connectivity between buildings in a campus environment to extend the reach of the LAN. These same advancements are being leveraged by wireless ISPs to extend their Point of Presence (POP) to neighborhoods that are without physical connectivity. An ISP extends its POP using wireless technology connecting its main office to an area. Then the ISP uses wireless technology from the subscriber's home to connect the subscriber to this wireless POP. You will see more and more of this type of service offering in the future, as the cost of this technology makes it affordable for regional ISPs to build and offer Internet services to highly populated areas.

Advances in cellular telephone networks are also taking place to address mobility and last mile issues pertaining to Internet expansion. Cellular technology, which emerged in the 1980s with the deployment of an analog network for voice communications, quickly expanded worldwide offering people mobility, and for some countries around the world, more accessible telephone service. You no longer had to wait for cables (last mile) to be brought to your home to have a phone. If there was a cell site, you had connectivity. I remember working in Mexico and there were places that took months and even years to get telephone lines added because of a lack of facilities from the government-controlled telephone company.

Cellular's success goes without saying. Just look around, and you are not likely to be too far from someone who has a cell phone, or you may even have one yourself, on your belt or in your purse. Early deployments of cellular services around the world were done with different standards and methods. Hence the early systems were unable to use the same telephone across the networks, particularly as you moved around the world. In the United States, the first cellular systems installed by competitors were of "like technology," and, as a result, "Roaming Arrangements," which were business relationships between the different cellular companies, allowed you to travel and have calls placed on a reciprocal network that billed to your cell number transparently. This created a mobility craze, and, I believe the start of "virtual culture" worldwide. I know that when cellular first came out and I purchased my first telephone for business, there were months when I was traveling that I had $1,300.00 phone bills, and this changed how I conducted business forever. I was no longer bound to the office. I could be in contact (wherever I had cellular coverage) with my employees, partners, customers, and vendors. With the later addition of a laptop computer (I purchased my first "laptop" in the mid 1980s, and I assure you it wasn't a laptop– perhaps a trunk top, as it was as big as a Samsonite hard-side suit case), I now had the first generation "virtual office." I could call and compute remotely, conducting business as needed between my Denver and San Diego offices as well as around the country to meet the needs of my customers who were located all over the United States. Life would never be the same again. It would be better in some ways, worse in others, and without question, a lot heavier when I traveled!

I was not the only person in the world who found this new freedom of mobility. It took the world by storm. As a result, a number of things happened, the first of which was over subscription and the need for more cellular capacity. This need gave rise to the next generation of cellular technology, which was digital Personal Communication System (PCS). Using digital technology and different frequencies, more subscribers could be put on the network. This increased revenues and extended the reach of wireless technology. This improvement of capacity and service features with the addition of text paging, web browsing, and instant messaging did, however, require the building of a new cellular infrastructure and the invention of new digital phones. Users who were early adopters of PCS services, which moved over from analog providers, were first attracted to PCS providers for the monthly savings caused by competition. I remember that my bill went down from $700.00 a month to below $200.00 each month—what a delight! Although this was not without cost. The robust national analog network we enjoyed over the years, which grew to have reliable coverage everywhere, was now back to the old days of "dead spots and dropped calls." It would only be a matter of time before this improved as PCS providers were installing more sites. And more importantly, the PCS providers came out with telephones that could support both analog and digital network connections. This means that you can have the benefits of digital service where it is available but the reach of the existing analog networks to make the service more functional.

I won't discuss the myriad of payment plans that went along with this new functionality, but it was a mind-bending experience. Nonetheless, at the end of the day, our bills were lower, and we were helping to pay for the expansion of the next generation of cellular services. Competition was truly the secret here as the FCC in the United States opened the licensing up to have six competitors in the PCS space for a market area. The analog world allowed only two, the wire line, which was at that time the RBOCs, and a "non-wire line," which were private independent competitors (i.e. Cellular One). This is important to keep in mind, because when we discuss satellite services later in the chapter, I will use this as a case study for the impending pricing model for satellite services.

I would also like to mention here that in the United States, roaming among the non-wire line providers was a little complicated until a man by the name of Craig McCaw went on the merger and acquisition trail, creating a company called Cellular One, which eventually created a competitive non-wire line solution to the RBOCs, making roaming and billing simpler. Now, I didn't say cheaper, because at that time, it was still very expensive, but it was, however, more competitive than the RBOCs. Craig later did one of the largest deals in communications history with the sale of his company Cellular One to AT&T. Sometime later, AT&T Wireless was born, and it still uses this network to augment its digital PCS systems. This is also very important, as I believe you will see a parallel story emerging in the satellite space, which I believe will be significant in the global expansion of the Internet. Stay tuned.

PCS providers are now moving to yet another generation of digital service, but this time, it will answer the business and personal need for connection to the global electronic marketplace. Up until now, very little was being done in the area of mobile data communications. First generation systems could only communicate for data services like our old 14.4k modems. Some current PCS systems have used compression to get this up to speeds of 56k similar to our 56k dial-up modems of today. But like the modems of today, this is not adequate for the requirements of tomorrow's Internet. Greater speed is required.

To accomplish higher speeds, the PCS networks need to be upgraded to what is referred to as 2G, 2.5G, and 3G networks. Basically, this refers to migration from first generation to second, third, and so on generations of PCS capabilities that offer broadband services, making connection to the Internet faster and more usable. This migration, which is taking place right now by most carriers around the world, is expensive, and for some, very complicated and cumbersome.

The cellular market worldwide could be characterized as fragmented. Most of Europe standardized to a technology called GSM, making it easier for users to enjoy the compatibility of their equipment with carriers all across the continent. Unity to this one standard has also allowed for easier deployment of mobile commerce applications and the security necessary to support such transactions.

In the United States technologies such as CDMA, TDMA, and GSM have been used by various carriers to build their networks. This fragmentation of networking technologies makes interoperability more complicated and expensive. It requires special telephones that support multiple bands or frequencies to leverage different network types. The most common example in the United States is a dual-band phone that can use the PCS digital and analog network automatically, depending on what is available. Digital is the first choice, with analog as the second choice, when there is a dead spot in the PCS digital network.

In addition, today's networks in the United States have been pieced together as a result of mergers and acquisitions of various companies endeavoring to gain subscribers and extend their reach. Having a more robust network with further reach and more subscribers gives carriers leverage to offer service and pricing plans that will help reduce "churn." Churn is the loss of customers to another carrier for whatever reason. In this game, the key is retention of subscribers—which represent your revenue streams.

This pieced-together network architecture has made billing and migration to next-generation networks a real challenge for the incumbent wireless carriers. Companies with networks using various technologies have a very choppy and non-backward compatible migration path. This means that as they introduce their new 2.5G and 3G offering, it will require extensive common equipment upgrades and telephone handset replacements. This need to change phones may make the adaptation slower, or worse, it could create churn, something a carrier doesn't want after spending large sums of money to update its networks.

Migration is also more complicated, creating less speed in the early stages for carriers that are forced to integrate more legacy systems into the equation. The old rule of "least common denominator" applies here because you are trying to balance the need of the new with the capability of the old. I would really hate to be a carrier in these times with such tough decisions needing to be made. Time is also not a carrier's friend, because the need for connectivity is marching on and placing great pressure on carriers to build out for fear of loss of subscribers.

Carriers that constructed their digital PCS networks from scratch after the first generation of analog cellular are better positioned for rapid deployment and smooth migration to 2.5 and 3G systems. By starting out with next-generation technologies, which are in adherence to the emerging global standard for wireless communications, these carriers may have gained competitive advantage. Upgrading their systems from 2G to 3G is a more direct path of migration. The migration path is also smoother, allowing backward compatibility of equipment, which provides a better value proposition for both the carrier and their subscribers. This investment protection is a critical advantage when the trend in the industry is reduced revenues from each subscriber because of the competitive nature of the wireless market. Revenue growth will come with the addition of more subscribers because of increased system capacity and the addition of "value-added features" now available with these next-generation networks.

The main purpose of migration to second- and third-generation networks is twofold. First, adding additional capacity to existing networks will allow more subscribers to be placed on the carrier's infrastructure, thus increasing the carrier's revenue base. Second, redesigning the network so that it can transport voice and data information in a converged optimized architecture will capture revenues derived by leveraging the craze of the Internet and its global electronic marketplace. To date, the killer application for cellular has been voice, but with recent worldwide trends, more data communications are now being carried on the telecommunications infrastructure than those of voice. As a result, carriers must upgrade to handle data transmission.

The upgrade to this new architecture will also facilitate higher speeds, which will be used to provide multimedia functionality to the wireless networks. This dovetails into the visual media section, assuring that people on the move will have full-motion video information available to them so that they can receive news broadcasts and collaborate with peers around the world. All types of services will be developed and deployed using this new infrastructure, including gaming, entertainment, financial, and communications applications. This will be a secured environment, leveraging digital technology and new security practices, which will emerge out of the financial and security industries to facilitate global e-commerce.

New mobile devices or appliances will be created so that users no longer have to be connected to their PC to have a full color multimedia-rich experience. This will serve to be a functional last- mile connection for many people who find themselves in transit, living life, and/or doing their job. With further developments of the PCS cellular network, you may even find carriers offering this type of services to homes for last mile connectivity. This will be most dependent on the network's ability to carry the wireless subscriber's mobile traffic (i.e., handset, PDA, laptop). Any excess capacity in an area could be used for such home connections. In any case the cellular mobile network will continue to be a key means for communications in the end-time theater.

Another key method in delivering last mile connectivity in the upcoming years and during the end-time theater is satellite communications. Satellite technology has been successfully used for years and has had great impact on our society. Satellites have been used for a variety of purposes including communications for telephone calling; data transmissions; broadcast TV and radio; scientific purposes of weather prediction; location; navigation and guidance systems (GPS); spy surveillance (national security); and, I am sure, many more that we don't know about.

The Star Wars Program, more appropriately defined as our missile defense system from space, was another potential use for satellite technology. It was thought that if there were a major launch, the systems could detect and destroy the Intercontinental Ballistic Missiles (ICBMs) before they would re-enter the earth's atmosphere. The satellite defense systems would be relatively safe from enemy attack because of their location in space. Only nations with such technology could impact this defense system by launching such an attack, and the very act of the attack, in and of itself, would serve as an early warning system, allowing a retaliatory strike prior to the ICBMs making landfall.

The recent war on terrorism commenced with a satellite launch prior to the major air initiative and ground movement. I suspect that the United States placed this satellite for the purpose of surveillance and guidance of new advanced weaponry. It was just a matter of fact, it needed to happen, the satellite was ready, they launched the bird (nickname for a satellite) and poof! They had eyes right where they needed them. *I thought this just exemplified what it is to be a superpower.* Only the Lord knows how many people this type of technology will save, keeping them from harm's way in war and allowing for good intelligence and surgically accurate air strikes.

Our special forces soldiers on the ground are using advanced satellite communications for voice, data, and video communications, sending secured information back to commanders all around the world or even to the President of the United States, anywhere he might be located. These systems are invincible unless an enemy can attack the communication satellite, unless, of course, the handheld device runs out of batteries. Batteries are still the "true plight" of the free world. If you travel frequently and need to stay connected you understand what I mean. Our ground troops can communicate via satellite telephone, handheld computing devices, and video telephones—I wonder if they are using the Iridium system that was recently saved by the government when Iridium Satellite LLC executives declared that they could not afford to keep the network running and asked the FCC if they could let the birds fall out of orbit and burn up as they reentered the earth's atmosphere.

I am glad that Iridium Satellite LLC, the venture capital firm that purchased the assets out of bankruptcy for the bargain price of $25 million, saved this S5 billion network of 64 LEO satellites. It would have been a waste to trash something that was functional and so monolithic (it was the first LEO satellite network in the world offering global phone and paging coverage).

Before their acquisition of the network, and the recent government bailout contract for $72 million (with options to extend to $252 million until 2007)[xiv], it was very expensive and was not optimized for high-speed data traffic. Today it still offers only a small value (if you're desperate) for data communications at speeds of 2-10 kbps, but the cost has gone down to $1.50 per minute[xv] making it available to the globe trotter and not just to the wealthy or the eccentric. To put today's monthly cost in perspective I use between 900 and 2,000 minutes per month when I am on the road, which would be $1,350.00-$3,000.00 per month, respectively, if I were using Iridium. If you are a globetrotter and need to be reached based on the value of your time, this may not be too high a monthly cost, considering the fact that you can be reached anywhere on the planet.

I remember when my wife Jan and I were on our millennium Carnival cruise, which I talked about early in the book (I did this to make a political statement against all of the hype of Y2K while serving as the Director of Communications at my firm), we were with a New York physician that we met on the ship, and he used the original Iridium satellite phone with great style. It looked as large as an old military field radio that you might see in a World War II movie, but it worked great, even out in the middle of the ocean! Hi, mom!

The Iridium project has fallen under some criticism because of its recent financial plight, thus may reflect negatively on the premise of global satellite networks being used for last mile connectivity, providing a converged architecture for multimedia communications, including voice, data, and video content. I think this is a shame, because it is a good idea, and Motorola is a great company.

The challenges faced by the original owner of the Iridium network revolve around a few key points. First Motorola (Iridium, LLC) was the first to focus on a global satellite system, attempting to address the roaming problems of the "globe trotting road warrior." At the time this network was conceived and created, the "killer application for mobility" was still voice calling and paging, as the convergence of data communications because of the reach of the Internet had not come to the forefront.

The architecture for this network supported voice, text paging, and slow-speed data communications, but it cannot provide broadband high-speed communications needed for multimedia communications. This, by example, illustrates the second problem, which is market evolution. Moore's law for 30 years has illustrated that technology doubles in speed and reduces by half in cost every 18 months. I believe that times have changed with the advent of the Internet and the pressure to quickly reach expanding global commerce markets. Some have said that an Internet year is 4-6 to six months, then technology changes or improves to make it yet "faster, cheaper, better" to meet a company's objective of "fast time to market."

Motorola's Iridium is basically a casualty of being a visionary with a great idea but one that simply got destroyed from being there just a little too early. It is said that invention is all about timing. You can have the greatest idea in the world, but if no one is ready for it, or if it gets leaped by something new or better, "you lose." Well, there you have it. The pressure for broadband high-speed wireless networks has basically made the voice-only Iridium network obsolete before it could get profitable. Without the bankruptcy sale, which reorganized the debt structure from $5 billion plus to $25 million, it could never cash flow. Now the new owners, having secured government contracts, which cover operating cost, can focus on commercial markets to make the network profitable. Brilliant play!

Another known issue with Motorola is their marketing. They are simply not that good at marketing. When you have a reputation for building the highest quality radio products in the world, you rest on reputation to carry your message. Well, it is a brave new world, and you need to tell your story. In addition, the speed of market movement creating competitive pressure in the mobility space made it less plausible for people to pay $3.00 per minute for service and more than $3,000.00 for a handset. It had to be more affordable.

I have discussed this because I know that as time moves on, there will be discussions about this subject and resistance to the mass development of global satellite networks as a result of this case study. I wanted you to have some perspective, because this will happen. It is just a matter of time.

Wireless Technology, the Next Frontier

The sky or wireless technology is the future of the communications industry for a few reasons. First, new networks can be engineered to meet today and tomorrow's Internet needs. The need, which these new emerging satellite networks will fulfill, is the ability to rapidly provide last mile expansion and a converged networking infrastructure that will be used for voice and multimedia visual communications anywhere in the world, as discussed in previous chapters.

The issue of engineering is important, because to practically blend all of these communications methods (voice, data and video) into one system network, you need to incorporate what is called "Quality of Service" (QOS). In layman's terms, as the subject is complex, it gives the equipment the ability to identify the contents of the data packet and route it in a way conducive to successfully completing the call or data transmission. A packet is like an electronic envelope used by devices that are responsible for delivering your content from your location to the desired end destination. The data packet, much like a physical envelope that you address and mail, has a source address (return address), a destination address (your intended party), and the contents.

To electronically add intelligence to the packet for proper delivery (routing), there is "header information." This header information is very important for QOS because it is used to identify, to the routing equipment, the payload contents, which could be voice information from a telephone call, data sent like e-mail, a video conversation using visual media, or streaming video multimedia content like a news broadcast. In converged networking, this is critical because of nature of the content being delivered, voice and video calls, which interact with your eyes and ears, and data payloads, which interact with other computers. QOS lets packets including voice and video payloads (which have timing issues associated with delivery, as people will want to hear each word you say in the order that you say them and/or see your lips move in sync with your voice clearly in a video conference), be routed in front of data packets, which can be delivered in "non-real time." Hopefully, I have adequately expressed this concept, as it could fill an entire book. I will not spend more time on this, but it is technically a cornerstone issue for the redesign of new satellite networks and the retrofit of existing legacy terrestrial and wireless cellular networks wishing to converge information for tomorrow's global electronic marketplace.

The second reason that satellite and wireless are the future for communications is their speed to market. The growing demand for connectivity can no longer wait on the time it takes to "sling cable or fiber" around the world to your last mile destination. The world is spinning toward this global electronic marketplace like nothing ever before in the history of mankind. We will discuss in the next chapter on e-commerce why the expansion of the Internet is occurring so quickly. Only wireless can address this type of rapid expansion, because it simply requires a small dish or wireless-equipped devices that are compatible with the system you are using for connectivity. With this connection, you will be able to leverage all that the Internet and this global community has to offer—information, entertainment, financial services, commerce opportunities, and on and on.

The third reason is strategic for the end-time theater. Satan, who is the "Prince of this world" (John 14:30) and "ruler of the air" (Ephesians 2:2) knows God's plan. He has read the Bible and knows it well (well enough to quote it when he needs to). He knows that his days are limited, and soon he will be unrestrained from ruling the earth during the last 3½ years of the Tribulation when God casts out Satan from the heavens and lifts his covering from the Earth as he pours out his wrath in full measure on the Earth in judgment.

> "And there was war in heaven. Michael and his angels fought against the dragon, and the dragon and his angels fought back. But he was not strong enough, and they lost their place in heaven. The great dragon was hurled down—that ancient serpent called the devil, or Satan,

who leads the whole world astray. He was hurled to the earth, and his angels with him. Then I heard a loud voice in heaven say: "Now have come the salvation and the power and the kingdom of our God, and the authority of his Christ. For the accuser of our brothers, who accuses them before our God day and night, has been hurled down. They overcame him by the blood of the Lamb and by the word of their testimony; they did not love their lives so much as to shrink from death. Therefore rejoice, you heavens and you who dwell in them! But woe to the earth and the sea, because the devil has gone down to you! He is filled with fury, because he knows that his time is short." (Revelation 12:7-12).

He also knows that God will judge the world with seismic activity (earthquakes) during the Tribulation as predicted.

"I watched as he opened the sixth seal. There was a great earthquake. The sun turned black like sackcloth made of goat hair, the whole moon turned blood red, and the stars in the sky fell to earth, as late figs drop from a fig tree when shaken by a strong wind. The sky receded like a scroll, rolling up, and every mountain and island was removed from its place. Then the kings of the earth, the princes, the generals, the rich, the mighty, and every slave and every free man hid in caves and among the rocks of the mountains. They called to the mountains and the rocks, "Fall on us and hide us from the face of him who sits on the throne and from the wrath of the Lamb! For the great day of their wrath has come, and who can stand?" (Revelation 6:12-17).

And as a result, Satan is motivating men to develop infrastructure that will be resilient against such devastation and disruption during these last days. Physical earthquakes do not disrupt wireless technology, particularly satellite communications, in the same way that terrestrial last mile service is disrupted. In the case of satellite communications, primary disruption would come with the destruction of the ground stations, which upload and download information to other Earth locations. Connection with the satellites can continue with a comprehensive network of backup Earth stations.

In addition, new design methods for the LEO systems are using distributed architecture (much like cellular mobile networks) relying less on ground stations and allowing direct communications with satellites that connect users to other wireless provisioned locations without the need of ground stations. I think we will see more and more movement to the dependency of satellite communications as the backbone infrastructure between locations.

Today we are very dependent on terrestrial fiber-optic backbones for connectivity around the globe. Carriers that depend heavily on terrestrial lines (copper and fiber-optic) buried in the ground and under the sea will suffer massive losses as the world is ravaged by physical disturbances. Time, which will seem like a precious commodity during these days of judgment, will not exist in sufficient quantities to quickly rebuild these physical last mile connections needed to communicate with and control the buying and selling done by the world's remaining inhabitants. Satan knows this and is preparing accordingly, because last mile connectivity is critical to the successful use of the electronic marketplace, which will control buying and selling by requiring a mark. I believe the mark will be electronic in nature (a chip based implant) and capable of leveraging such a computing infrastructure—the very infrastructure used today by the financial community worldwide. The Bible says:

> "He was given power to give breath to the image of the first beast, so that it could speak and cause all who refused to worship the image to be killed. He also forced everyone, small and great, rich and poor, free and slave, to receive a mark on his right hand or on his forehead, so that no one could buy or sell unless he had the mark, which is the name of the beast or the number of his name. This calls for wisdom. If anyone has insight, let him calculate the number of the beast, for it is man's number. His number is 666." (Revelation 13:16-17).

I believe that as you watch the development of wireless technology, the race for space, and the deployment of wireless appliances, (which we are growing dependent on for communications and doing our jobs) this premise will speak for itself. Convergence of chip-based technologies used for identification and financial purposes, securing transactions over these wireless networks, will also become more prevalent because of recent world terrorism events, which are creating a global fear in the people and governments of the Earth.

Currently the development of satellite systems capable of delivering this type of global connectivity reads like the Who's Who of the communications and technology industries. I have never seen such a race for space nor the associated challenges with building such networks. We have many functional satellites providing broadcast TV and data communications, but there have been some false starts in the area of global communications. I think this will continue until someone gets the vision and acts upon this vision for building a network optimized for converged Internet services allowing for secured voice, data, and multimedia communications. The network should have the ability to provide mobile and fix-based last mile connections with sufficient capacities for rapid expansion into every market of the world, especially those located in the regions of the end-time theater, which includes Europe, the Middle East, Russia, and Asia. The role of the United States is unclear in prophecy, although we are heavily involved with Middle East policy today and act as a strong ally for Israel.

Just to digress for a moment, capacity is an interesting issue, because it will take care of itself in the last days. Networks will be built today anticipating a growing global economy, but as judgments occur, the population of the world will be greatly reduced (by billions), making it possible to provide connectivity to everyone left on the Earth with such systems.

Companies and investors such as Alcatel, Motorola, Hughes, Teledesic, Matra Marconi Space, Boeing, Lockheed Martin, Loral Space & Communications, Abu Dhabi Investment Company, Liberty Media, Astrolink, Intelsat, Skybridge LP, Craig McCaw, Bill Gates and Saudi Prince Alwaleed Bin Talal are lining up to get into the game. In this race for space and the last mile connection, these companies will simultaneously spend billions of dollars on the development of satellite networks.

Emerging Low Earth Orbit (LEO) satellite technology is addressing the issue of latency (the delay in delivering data packets) by moving the satellites 25 times closer to Earth than those of geostationary-type technology, which was used in the past. Geostationary-Earth-orbit (GEO) systems are placed at an altitude of 36,000 kilometers above the equator in comparison to non-geostationary-Earth-orbit (LEO) systems, which are placed at an altitude of about 750-1300 kilometers. This closer proximity to the Earth will give a projected 30-millisecond (ms) propagation time for the data transport. To put this in perspective, private networks today have 30-50 ms response times, and the Internet is functioning at 85-250 ms, depending on the type of service, and the time of day. The LEO satellite technology decrease in latency is critical, because to do converged networking based on today's compression technology, you need to stay under 150ms for voice calls to be delivered successfully with toll quality. Adding 30 ms of overhead to today's current transport speeds would not likely impact packet delivery, especially if the users were on the same network provider, using similar technology. This more direct path through space will provide speeds equal to today's high-speed fiber-optic network backbones but have the ability to be placed anywhere in the world without limitations of physical wiring, giving these solutions a distinct advantage over those of terrestrial facilities and carriers.

The following diagram illustrates various satellite orbits relevant to their proximity to the Earth. Notice how much closer the LEO satellite orbits are in comparison to others. This reduces latency and improves transmission quality for time sensitive data payloads like voice or video conferencing conversations. The diagram is used by permission from Lloyd's satellite constellation.[xvi]

Orbital altitudes for satellite constellations
▬ peak radiation bands of the Van Allen belts (high-energy protons)
orbits are not shown at actual inclination; this is a guide to altitude only
from Lloyd's satellite constellations http://www.ee.surrey.ac.uk/Personal/L.Wood/constellations/

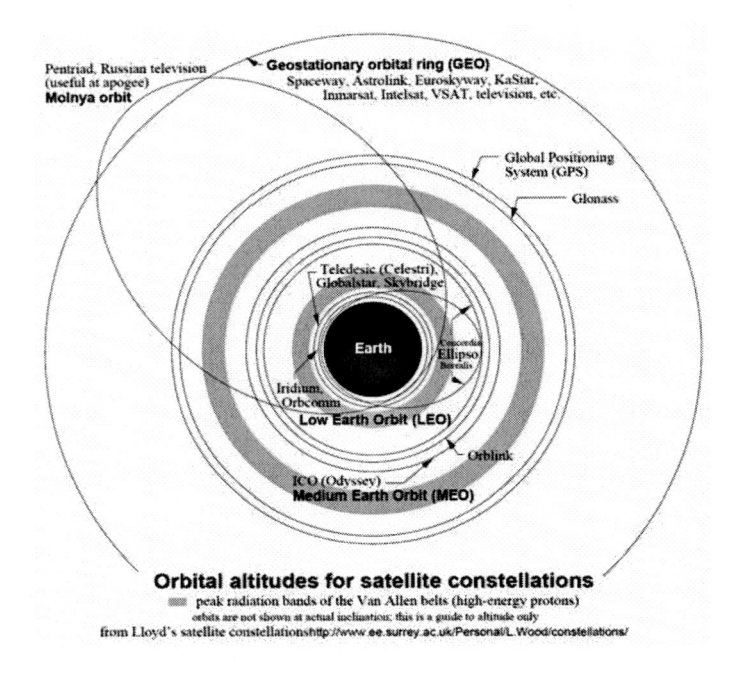

The scope of the build out, which has been under way since the early 1990s with the commencement and assignment of licensing for use of the wireless spectrum, is shaping up to be a unique race. My eyes were on the company called Teledesic, which is owned primarily by Craig McCaw, a leader in the wireless market, along with investors such as Bill Gates, Saudi Prince Alwaleed Bin Talal, Abu Dhabi Investment Company, The Boeing Company, and Motorola. Their intent was to launch the world's largest LEO satellite network. The company's original plans included 288 operational satellites, divided into 12 planes, each with 24 satellites. This would make efficient use of the radio spectrum. Frequencies would be allocated dynamically and would be capable of being reused many times to increase the system capacity. The revised design, which was awarded to satellite manufacturer Alenia Spazio SpA in early 2002, included the first two, of a planned 30-satellite constellation.

"The system a Global, Broadband Internet-in-the Sky ™ Network blends the coverage and low latency of a LEO constellation of satellites, the flexibility and robustness of the Internet and "fiber-like" Quality of Service (QOS) to bring affordable access to interactive broadband communications to all areas of the Earth including those areas that could not be served economically by any other means." This paragraph describing the system came from the Teledesic website and is dead on target. This is exactly the technical vision and economic outlook a solution like this need to address the demands of the global electronic marketplace that is developing around us.

The players in this investment have the know-how, the financial wherewithal, and the motives to successfully create a converged wireless transport solution. Craig McCaw is Mr. Wireless, having made billions on the AT&T merger when he sold Cellular One to them at the launch of the PCS wireless craze. Bill Gates has a simple view–put his software on every device in the universe and make it accessible on any device "anywhere, anytime, and all the time." What better match than to invest in the wireless infrastructure game? Now he can influence design initiatives and adapt his software to leverage wireless transport. This is key, because the network needs to be usable for people, impacting their lives at work and play. Plumbing (or pipes, which the industry refers to as networking infrastructure) is useless unless it carries applications that are usable by business and consumers. Microsoft will make sure that the applications are there, and McCaw will build the pipes. His other investors are also strategic because they build satellite systems, maintain them, and develop radio equipment. He has a complete team assembled.

Unfortunately, on September 30, 2002 Teledesic announced the suspension of work on the construction of their satellite network. The press release quotes CEO Craig McCaw saying, "We have met our regulatory milestones to date and remain financially solvent. Our decision to suspend our activities results from an unprecedented confluence of events in the telecommunications industry and financial markets. We do not presently see elements in place that would result in returns to our shareholders that are commensurate with the risk. We continue to believe that the Teledisic service would ultimately provide unique and measurable benefits to the world, and we are looking at scenarios to preserve the ability for that service to be realized." Well, I agree with you Craig, your service would provide unique and measurable benefits to the world. I cannot wait for you to find the right scenario.

There are other emerging relationships such as Alcatel's Skybridge, Globalstar, Thuraya, ICO Global Communications (acquired by Craig McCaw), Ellipso (collaborating with ICO), and ORBCOMM that are competing for the same marketplace—wireless last mile. These players have big investors, have satellite manufacturers as partners, and are very capable of making this happen. The fact that many are competing for the market also means that pricing will be very affordable, much like that of the cellular industry when local markets were opened up to six providers rather than two. This is important, because we no longer have time to wait for connectivity, because of artificially imposed pricing constraints by carriers that control a unique global network offering. The fear of loss of market share by these players is driving them to be there first and to make it affordable. LEO technology, in comparison to previous satellite architectures, is said to be more cost effective to build and deploy, which should help the financial picture in this large undertaking.

I also believe, just like Iridium was saved by the United States Department of Defense, that these networks will be built—right, wrong, or indifferent—because they need to be to constructed to complete the readiness of the world for end-time events. As a result, men will be blinded by their aspirations and motivations to build such solutions, as they clearly represent the fortunes of the next decade. It is easy to use the sins of our past to drive men to conclusion. Pride, covetousness, idolatry, and greed have been used by Satan for thousands of years to accomplish his purposes on earth. Nothing is different today. Let me say here, as this is a key focal point for the future, that I am not saying that these men are evil or possessed by the devil or anything of the like. Rather, I am saying that the world and all of its inhabitants are part of a larger picture that has been going on since the dawn of man. This battle, which has been raging since the fall of mankind in the garden with Satan's temptation of Eve and the subsequent fall of Adam, is all about Satan's pride and his desire to be worshiped like the most high God.

It is a battle for your soul against an enemy whose only desire is to hunt, kill, and destroy the mankind created by God. Satan will have his final hour, and he is preparing things right now for these events so that he can control mankind and force the worship of himself in the last days. The good news in all of this is that we know the outcome. Jesus Christ defeated Satan forever when He, while we were yet sinners, submitted Himself to death on the cross to pay the penalty for our sins and to make a way for us to return to God the Father in Heaven. God said in John 3:16: "For God so loved the world that he gave his one and only Son, that whoever believes in him shall not perish but have eternal life."

We have the promise of everlasting life when we place our faith in the finished work of Jesus Christ on the cross of Calvary. The Bible says that when Jesus had completed His work of sacrifice on the cross for all the sins of mankind, He said, "It is finished," and He gave up his spirit and died. Men did not kill Jesus Christ. They only did what men do. God sent Jesus to the Earth to be a living sacrifice that could satisfy God's requirement for a blood sacrifice for sin. And Jesus went willingly to the cross, in obedience and out of love for His creation, to pay the price for sin and to defeat death so that men can have eternal life.

Friends, this is personal, and it is for you as an individual. Psalm 139 says that God knows who you are by name, that while you were in the womb, He knew you and formed you. He knows your ways. He knows everything about you and he cares for you, enough to sacrifice his only Son. Jesus would have died just for you, even if you were the only person on this Earth. It is that personal! Jesus just says to receive as a free gift, with the faith of a child, the gift of eternal life made available through asking Him to come into your heart and be your God, Savior, Lord, and Friend. Ephesians 3:8-9 says, "For by grace are you saved through faith, it is not of yourselves, it is a gift of God, not of works lest any man should boast."

This is an important contrast, because our loving Creator has given mankind a choice, or free will. It started in the Garden of Eden with a tree, the tree of the knowledge of good and evil, and God said that Adam and Eve could eat everything else, but not the fruit of this one tree. He told them that if they ate from it, they would "surely die." He was very clear and precise. There was no confusion or ambiguity. We can depend on God to be faithful to what He says. He is unchanging. Well, Eve was deceived by Satan's subtle twist: "You will not surely die" and ate the fruit. In so doing, she chose death. And here we are today, reaping the outcome. Satan in the last days will not be a god of free will and choice. He will, as we have seen prophesied in the Bible, force mankind to worship him by receiving his mark or be killed. Events taking place in the world today in the areas of the economy, government, technology, transportation, health and welfare, human rights, and peacemaking efforts are all part of an elaborate plan. Jesus Christ will one day return to the Earth from the sky with the heavenly hosts and claim his rightful place as Lord, King, and Judge of mankind. The Bible says He will come as a thief in the night, surprising us, because "No one knows about that day or hour, not even the angels in heaven, nor the Son, but only the Father" (Matthew 24:36-51). So we are encouraged to be ready.

Dependencies and Holdouts

Communications are at the foundation of all of the things we have discussed in this book and are a critical component to the readiness of the infrastructure to support the end-time events of Revelation, Chapter 13, which will require all of mankind to receive a mark so that they can buy and sell goods and services, basically to live as we know it today if you are in the developed free world.

This issue of the last mile and the ability to connect the inhabitants (or as I mentioned earlier, the remaining inhabitants) of the Earth to this electronic marketplace is a real challenge today and I believe the final technology holdout to accomplish what needs to be done to fulfill this prophecy of things to come. Most areas—financial, visual media, and security industries—are ready or at the brink of global release of the solutions to support topics discussed in this book. I think the explosion will come and all things will tie together when the communications infrastructure is prepared to support this global electronic marketplace.

I want to leave you with these thoughts, which are relevant to this section of the book. The key is global connectivity that can be rapidly and inexpensively deployed, which has little impact from global disturbances like weather and earthquakes and can be quickly reconnected in the event of disruption without large dependencies on physical terrestrial infrastructure. This is critical, because the network connections need to be stable for Satan to be able to use the infrastructure effectively to control mankind and force you to worship him during the last 3½ years of the tribulation period.

On January 4, 2002, I picked up the newspaper and read about a "revolutionary" communications technology called Ultra-wideband. It was said that this technology, which uses radio energy versus radio waves, has been around for 20 years, but recently it has been improved to allow for the reutilization of various frequencies, called frequency hopping, to provide another broadband access methodology. The FCC has recognized this as revolutionary technology and has approved the use of the new method. Cellular telephone providers, those with GPS interests and the airline industry (air traffic controllers) are up in arms with this decision, because they say that the new system could interfere with transmissions in these frequency spectrums, causing problems with telephones, GPS location systems, and the safety systems used to control airliners around the world. Testing will soon commence to see if there is need for such worry.

This is the type of development I am talking about. I have discussed wireless telephony, satellite systems, and the like, because they are in the news today, but the bottom line is that something, possibly a technology that we have not yet discovered, will solve the last mile dilemma and make it possible for the inhabitants of this world to be connected anytime, anyplace, and all the time. A friend of mind, Bill Bryla (a specialized electronic technologist who tests radio emissions) once told me that he had a vision that God was going to give him revelation for a new revolutionary last mile technology unlike anything known to man today. Now I am not saying that he will develop this or that it will actually come to fruition, but just think. Here is a guy who is getting this type of notion from the Lord, and he just so happens to know a guy called to write a book on such a subject. I have seen God work in such ways, and I believe that around the world, He is providing people with such revelation.

Just read the technology rags and newspapers and watch the commercials. This is on the minds of everyone in our business. The Internet requires anytime, anywhere, all the time intelligently connected devices to connect us to this virtual global electronic marketplace that is being developed. With such an infrastructure, you will be able to communicate globally, get information, receive news broadcasting, play games, irrefutably identify yourself electronically, and most importantly, leverage the financial community to buy and sell goods and services electronically anywhere in the world. Everything we have discussed in this book so far is dependent on this sector of the technology industry. Without it, there is a void, an inability to fully progress. Hence the energy you see around the development and deployment of such technologies.

This brings me to a point of reflection of the current state of the industry and a close to this chapter. Recently in the marketplace, the technology industry, especially the telecommunications industry (or the communications industry as dubbed in this book), has taken many financial hits and setbacks in the stock market. In the late 1990s, these stocks were hot with the building of worldwide fiber networks, the expansion of ISPs worldwide, the construction of new wired and wireless networks, and the rise of new broadband providers. This industry sector was the talk of the town, or at least of Wall Street, with growth companies such as Cisco rising to fame during this period in history. Then, almost overnight, the industry started to have financial problems, fiber-optic networks were built but underutilized, data centers that were constructed for the expected worldwide expansion of the Internet were sitting empty, and broadband suppliers providing needed high-speed Internet connections to home and businesses were going out of business. How could this be? Everything points to the need of this type of infrastructure, so what is happening? Why are the satellite companies having so much challenge funding and constructing their much-needed global wireless systems? And why is there push back on the development and use of new revolutionary technologies?

I would love to tell you that I know the answer, but I don't! I know that what I have said is absolutely right on. We need and must have this infrastructure. And some day you will see it happen before your eyes. But it seems to be hitting the wall in these early years of the new millennium. I will offer this thought for your consideration. God, who is sovereign, and is the Creator and Ruler of the universe, is in control. He says that no man knows the day or the hour of the return of Jesus Christ to Earth but Himself, God alone. There is no question that these events will happen and that the end-time theater of the Book of Revelation will take place, but when these events happen is totally up to God the Father Himself.

Revelation, the last book of the Bible, is about judgment on mankind and the final return of Jesus Christ to establish his earthly kingdom and to rule on Earth as King and Lord. As a result, the only thing I can think of which may have stopped what seemed to be an "unstoppable force", by anything known to man, was an act of God's hand. God in response to the prayers of His people crying out, in repentance for the sins of the nations, changed the course of business progress. The Bible says: "If my people, who are called by my name, will humble themselves and pray and seek my face and turn from their wicked ways, then will I hear from heaven and will forgive their sin and will heal their land." (2 Chronicles 8:14) The Bible also says: "The prayer of a righteous man is powerful and effective. Elijah was a man just like us. He prayed earnestly that it would not rain, and it did not rain on the land for three and a half years. Again he prayed and the heavens gave rain, and the earth produced its crop." (James 5:16-17).

We could possibly be witnessing God using the economy and worldwide events to control the rollout of such technologies in answer to the prayers of believers in Jesus Christ all around the world who pray for God's forgiveness, mercy, and revelation to the world that Jesus is coming, and coming soon. This is the only thing I can imagine, based on what I know about the industry today.

Throughout the Bible, we have seen God respond to His people's prayers, sometimes the simple pleading of just one person, withholding judgment until a later time. I recall an account in the Old Testament. Moses had led the people of Israel out of Egypt, and upon their return to sin and idolatry (while Moses was on the mountain receiving the 10 commandments) and their lack of trust to go into the promised land, God decided to kill them in the desert and raise up a new people through Moses. Moses, heavy with this thought, cried out for the mercy of God and pleaded with Him, saying something like this: "God, please do not judge Your people here. Now, think of what will be said about You. It will be said that You led them out into the desert and then You killed Your people." God answered the prayers of Moses by withholding that immediate judgment and rather had the children of Israel wander in the desert until those who needed to be judged died by natural causes. Then those who were faithful to God's leading were able to enter the Promised Land as promised by God.

God hears our prayers and our cries for mercy. He heard them in the days of Moses, and He hears them today. Someday the world's sin and lack of repentance will bring God to the place where He will commence with the events prophesied in the Book of Revelation. Prior to this time, the business community will be allowed to accomplish building the needed infrastructure to support the end-time theater events described in Revelation, Chapter 13.

As of today, you still have time to get ready for the return of Jesus Christ, possibly because of the prayers of one person in your life, such as your mother, dad, friend, or pastor, or maybe even the prayers of people around the world who do not even know you but are pouring out their hearts earnestly for the lost souls of this world, pleading that God would wait and extend his mercy and love one more day to everyone, making Himself known to each and every individual who does not know Jesus Christ personally.

Do you know Him? Are you resting on His work alone on the cross? Is your name written in the Lamb's Book of Life? When you die, will you hear Him welcome you home as his son or daughter? Or will Jesus come to your life as a thief in the night? Will He surprise you and find you unready for His coming? Will you be living a life focused on yourself, your pleasures, and your material wealth? Or even worse, will you think you are ready, working and striving in your own power to be a good person, helping others, going to church, and thinking that your efforts can earn your way to Heaven? Jesus said, "I am the way and the truth and the life. No one comes to the Father except through me." (John 14:6).

If this is you, I encourage you to read Chapter 8 about how to have a personal relationship with Jesus Christ. It is faith in Him alone that can put you back in relationship with a Holy God, and that is as simple as receiving a free gift with the blind faith of a child. My prayer is that you will do this today and experience the fullness in your soul that only Jesus Christ can bring. The Bible says: "For God so loved the world that he gave his one and only Son, that whoever believes in him shall not perish but have eternal life." (John 3:16)

Notes:

[xiv] Iridium Satellite LLC web site press release, December 12, 2000.

[xv] *Convergence*, December 2001, page 37. Iridium advertisement showing a rate of $1.50 per minute, including roaming and long distance.

[xvi] Orbital altitudes for satellite constellations diagram, Lloyd's satellite constellations web site, February 2005, http://www.ee.surrey.ac.uk/Personal/L.Wood/constellations/

Chapter Six

Electronic Commerce—The New World Economy

The Evolution of Electronic Commerce—The "Killer Application"

In this chapter we will discuss the evolution of e-commerce as it relates to end-time prophecies. This is an important chapter, connecting the four previously discussed technology sectors together, completing the puzzle picture, and revealing the mystery of God for this unique time in the history of mankind.

The convergence of the four technology sectors enables the creation of global business applications, which will electronically make the selling and purchasing of goods and services easy and secure. In effect, the culmination of all of the technologies developed, the convergence of the various technology sectors, and the development of business applications, which leverage these industries, are becoming the "killer application" to enable the electronic globalization of our society connecting users anytime, anywhere, all the time. This notion of anytime, anywhere, and all the time is the focus of every major technology company in the industry, which focuses on providing e-services (electronic- or Internet-powered business applications).

As technologists we are constantly, within our industry specialties, seeking the killer application. The development of a killer application is like finding the Holy Grail. It is what all software developers seek when they sit down to the keyboard and begin to write code. This notion of creating an application that will impact the way we live in such a way that it becomes commonplace or a brand name is the ultimate achievement for someone in the technology industry.

Most companies or developers have traditionally looked at these killer applications as point solutions, which means that they focus on the development of an application that addresses a specific industry or problem. You might think of this as a niche market. As a result, each industry sector continues to search for the ultimate killer application that will give it dominance in its specific industry.

It has become my view, as a convergence architect, that this elusive search and drive for the ultimate killer application has been far more successful than many companies or individuals think. In fact, they have contributed in ways that they likely do not even realize, and such contributions are shaping the world at the very end of the current age of mankind's history, making way for the glorious return of our Lord and Savior Jesus Christ.

Convergence —A Climactic Symphony

I believe that the technology markets have been evolving simultaneously, converging together slowly over time, almost like a symphony, building climactically under the leadership of the conductor, to address the market demands of the global marketplace, creating the ultimate "killer application" as part of a plan that was predicted in the Bible thousands of years ago. The Bible predicted in the Book of Revelation, Chapter 13, that Satan would rise to power through a man who would become known in the Bible as the Antichrist. This world leader, who will be possessed by Satan himself, will rise to power, counterfeiting the things of God and Jesus Christ, including the ability to make world peace and do miracles. The Antichrist will even be resurrected, deceiving the inhabitants of the world and causing them to worship him. The result of this choice will be the full wrath and judgment of God and separation from Him for all of eternity.

> Revelation 14:9-11 says: "Then another angel, a third one, followed them, saying with a loud voice, "If anyone worships the beast and his image, and receives a mark on his forehead or on his hand, he also will drink of the wine of the wrath of God, which is mixed in full strength in the cup of His anger; and he will be tormented with fire and brimstone in the presence of the holy angels and in the presence of the Lamb." And the smoke of their torment

goes up forever and ever; they have no rest day and night, those who worship the beast and his image, and whoever receives the mark of his name."

This is a grim picture of things to come for those who are deceived by the Antichrist and the events taking place in the last days. The Bible says that in the last days, men will continue in their sin, they will follow the Antichrist, and, as a result of their choice not to repent, God will send strong delusion to their minds so that they are unable to discern the truth, and they will receive the full judgment of God for their sins. The Bible says: "Now we request you, brethren, with regard to the coming of our Lord Jesus Christ and our gathering together to Him, that you not be quickly shaken from your composure or be disturbed either by a spirit or a message or a letter as if from us, to the effect that the day of the Lord has come. Let no one in any way deceive you, for it will not come unless the apostasy comes first, and the man of lawlessness is revealed, the son of destruction, who opposes and exalts himself above every so-called god or object of worship, so that he takes his seat in the temple of God, displaying himself as being God. Do you not remember that while I was still with you, I was telling you these things? And you know what restrains him now, so that in his time he will be revealed. For the mystery of lawlessness is already at work; only he who now restrains will do so until he is taken out of the way. Then that lawless one will be revealed whom the Lord will slay with the breath of His mouth and bring to an end by the appearance of His coming; that is, the one whose coming is in accord with the activity of Satan, with all power and signs and false wonders, and with all the deception of wickedness for those who perish, because they did not receive the love of the truth so as to be saved. For this reason God will send upon them a deluding influence so that they will believe what is false, in order that they all may be judged who did not believe the truth, but took pleasure in wickedness. But we should always give thanks to God for you, brethren beloved by the Lord, because God has chosen you from the beginning for salvation through sanctification by the Spirit and faith in the truth. It was for this He called you through our gospel, that you may gain the glory of our Lord Jesus Christ." (2 Thessalonians 2:1-14).

Friends, this warning is clear. Satan will rise up and during the last days be unrestrained by God to do what he will with the Earth and mankind. The Bible is clear that men will be judged for their sins. And this passage says that God will even, in the last days, send delusion so that those who have not repented under the message of love will be fully judged. Jesus Christ is returning to Earth as the judge of mankind, and he will surprise many as a thief in the night when he returns in the clouds to defeat Satan for the last time in the battle of Armageddon and assumes his rightful place on Earth as Lord and King.

If you are reading this now, today is the day of salvation. The Bible says that God will reveal Himself to every man, making the message of Jesus Christ known so that everyone is without excuse. If you have been reading this book, you are without excuse. Jesus has used this to reveal His message to you. The question is: Will you accept His free gift of salvation as a result of His death, burial and resurrection? On that lonely cross, while we were yet sinners, he lovingly died for us–for me and for you. Jesus said: "I am the way and the truth and the life. No one comes to the Father except through me." (John 14:6).

We have all had the thought that life is short. You may even have had someone you loved snatched unexpectedly from your life because of a sudden illness or accident. We never know when death may knock on our door. So this is why today, right now, is the right time to receive Jesus Christ into your life. All you have to do is to pray and to ask Jesus to forgive you of your sins, tell Him that you want to receive His free gift of salvation through His work alone on the cross for you, and believe in your heart that He will do this, because the Bible says that He will. The Bible says: "That if you confess with your mouth Jesus as Lord, and believe in your heart that God raised Him from the dead, you will be saved; for with the heart a person believes, resulting in righteousness, and with the mouth he confesses, resulting in salvation." (Romans 10:9-10).

Waiting could be fateful in these last days, because things are evolving, and I believe that we could see the rise of the Antichrist anytime. Recent world events illustrate how small our world is. We are a global society. All it would take is a catastrophic event to drive the peoples of the Earth to band together under the banner of peace, security, or a charismatic leader who says all the right things and seemingly has the power to deliver on his promises. This leader would become the monarch of the world, controlling all of the kingdoms around the globe using the global technology infrastructure that is being implemented right now to become the most powerful killer application in the history of mankind. Little did we know that our search for the killer application would literally produce an application that would rob man of his very soul—killing him not just physically, but more importantly, spiritually.

As I have mentioned throughout the book, the Bible says that in the last days, it will be required that everyone on the Earth receive the mark of the Antichrist that signifies their allegiance and worship of him. In exchange, you will be able to buy and sell goods and services and live life as we know it today. The Bible says (*comments in italics added by author for clarity*):

> "Then I saw another beast coming up out of the earth; and he had two horns like a lamb and he spoke as a dragon (*the Antichrist's lieutenant*). He exercises all the authority of the first beast

(*the Antichrist*) in his presence. And he makes the earth and those who dwell in it to worship the first beast (*the Antichrist*), whose fatal wound was healed. He performs great signs, so that he even makes fire come down out of heaven to the earth in the presence of men. And he deceives those who dwell on the earth because of the signs which it was given him to perform in the presence of the beast, telling those who dwell on the earth to make an image to the beast who had the wound of the sword and has come to life. And it was given to him to give breath to the image of the beast, so that the image of the beast would even speak and cause as many as do not worship the image of the beast to be killed. And he causes all, the small and the great, and the rich and the poor, and the free men and the slaves, to be given a mark on their right hand or on their forehead, and he provides that no one will be able to buy or to sell, except the one who has the mark, either the name of the beast or the number of his name. Here is wisdom. Let him who has understanding calculate the number of the beast, for the number is that of a man; and his number is six hundred and sixty-six." (Revelation 13:11-18).

The false prophet (the Antichrist's lieutenant) will create an idol of some sort that even has the ability to speak and require everyone to worship this idol or to be killed. This would be easy with technology today. A visual image of the Antichrist could appear on the screen of a handheld computer, a laptop, a TV, a cash register, or a visual financial portal prior to the sale or purchase of anything asking for your pledge of allegiance and worship. With speech recognition technology and voice printing (this is like fingerprinting your voice) it could even be interactive and/or validate with your voice response of your worship. This is as simple to do as the windows splash screen that comes on every time you turn on your computer. It even plays you a nice little tune. Perhaps the phrase of the future will be, "Do you love and worship me?" Be careful how you answer, because it will cost you more than just your physical life. It will cost you your eternal life and your very soul.

The mark of the beast, which will be required to be taken by every man, small and great, rich and poor, free and slave, will be used in conjunction with this practice of idolatry to control the buying and selling of goods and services. When the time comes, the Antichrist will require all men, without being a respecter of persons, to have his mark. He will not be a god of free will, letting you chose whether you love him or not, but he will be a controlling monarch who will use the very threat of you being "turned off" in society, denying you of the very basics of life—food, shelter, clothing.

Think of this. Sometime in the not too distant future, we will become a global electronic culture with secure access to the electronic network anytime, anywhere, all the time. We will depend on and use this technology in restaurants, airports, gas stations, hospitals, grocery stores, and banks, literally everywhere that you transact business. And now, all of a sudden, you cannot sell or purchase anything without making a choice to worship this new leader. The network has also become the backbone for communications one to another, allowing you to talk on the phone, send e-mail, instant message one another, video conference, and receive visual broadcasting of content of all types. Basically, it has become woven into the fabric of your life, slowly, subtly, and with great purpose and deliberation.

Unfortunately, as a result of such a well executed plan, based on the knowledge of mankind and their weaknesses, fears, and personal desires, many will fall into the trap of taking this mark under the justification of "I have no choice. I have to receive the mark to continue living life. What choice do I have?" Others may also believe in the Antichrist because of the things he has done for the "good of mankind" during the first 3½ years of the Tribulation period (the Tribulation is the 7 year period of judgment prophesied in the Bible prior to the final return of Jesus Christ to Earth), creating what seems to be world peace in the Middle East and around the world. (Bringing peace to the Middle East, in and of itself, will seem like a miracle, considering how long we have been watching and listening to this group of "hard heads" battling over this holy piece of dirt. By the way, I can say this because I am one of those hard heads. This group of followers may simply believe and choose to worship him as a deity because they love what he says, what he stands for, and what he empowers them to do in this new world. Everything he says will "feel good." It will make sense, because it appeals to the sin nature of man. The Antichrist will speak tolerance in morals and in religion (until he mandates you to worship him), but for some reason, this will still seem to make sense to people. He will encourage sin and sexual pleasure and will feed your eyes with content that gives rise to the lust of the flesh. The Antichrist will know how to push your buttons and how to tempt you.

I could spend a great deal of time, on this but all you need to do is to look around in society and you will see a decay of morals, the decline in the belief of God, and a relentless pursuit of things that gratify self, which has become the idolatry of our time. It is the spirit of always needing more, never being content with what we have–always needing a nicer car, a bigger home, nicer clothes, a higher paying job, a more beautiful or handsome mate, or more sex. You name it. The theme is "more is better." As I mentioned earlier, the Bible says that such a choice to follow the Antichrist and receive his mark will lead to the judgment of God in your life, separating you from Him for eternity and committing your soul to the torment of hell and suffering forever.

In contrast, the first time Jesus came to Earth, He came as a suffering servant, as a loving, substitutionary sacrifice to die for your sins, as a way to reconcile you back to a holy and righteous God, so that **by choice, by faith, and without force, you could choose** to invite him into your life and receive the free gift of eternal life. His "second coming," when He reveals Himself to the peoples of the Earth, will be triumphant. It will be bold. And He will come in the sky with the army of the heavenly hosts. He will ride a white horse. Jesus will be dressed in white with an inscription on his robe that reads "King of Kings and Lord of Lords."

> "I saw heaven standing open and there before me was a white horse, whose rider is called Faithful and True. With justice he judges and makes war. His eyes are like blazing fire, and on his head are many crowns. He has a name written on him that no one knows but he himself. He is dressed in a robe dipped in blood, and his name is the Word of God. The armies of heaven were following him, riding on white horses and dressed in fine linen, white and clean. Out of his mouth comes a sharp sword with which to strike down the nations. "He will rule them with an iron scepter." He treads the winepress of the fury of the wrath of God Almighty. On his robe and on his thigh he has this name written: **"KING OF KINGS AND LORD OF LORDS."** (Revelation 19:11-16).

This time Jesus will come first as judge, defeating the armies of Satan and the inhabitants of the Earth who have chosen to worship the Antichrist and have received his mark. Then He will establish His kingdom on Earth and take His rightful place as King of Kings and Lord of Lords. There will be no mistaking this event, friends. No one will miss the return of Jesus Christ to Earth to judge mankind during his final appearing. Unlike the first time when Jesus was painfully despised and rejected by mankind as prophesied in the Old Testament, this time many who know Him personally will be watching for His glorious appearing. And those who are not watchful, who do not know him as Savior, will unmistakably know Him as their judge.

So what is the punch line? Know Jesus Christ personally and receive Him into your life today, because no man knows the day or the hour that Jesus will return to Earth, nor do you know when your life will be over. Also, please understand what Jesus Christ **will not look like** when he returns to Earth the second time. He **will not** appear as a man doing great miracles trying to establish an earthly utopia. He will not be an earthly deity, an earthly leader declaring Himself as God and establishing Himself in the reconstructed Solomon's Temple in Jerusalem. This will be Satan himself, a false Christ, so do not be deceived. The Bible says that in the last days, there will be many who will try to say that they are the Christ or a prophet: "At that time if anyone says to you, 'Look, here is the Christ!' or, 'Look, there he is!'

do not believe it. For false Christs and false prophets will appear and perform signs and miracles to deceive the elect—if that were possible. So be on your guard; I have told you everything ahead of time." (Mark 13:21-23).

So, where are we in the development of the ultimate killer application? How far along is the creation of this electronic global network that will enable Satan to control the inhabitants of the Earth? Is it really possible to use technology to control the buying and selling of goods and services worldwide? And what would it take to accomplish this? Well, my answer is simple, but it is in the form of a question that I pose to you. Look around, and based on the things that you have learned in the previous chapters; the condition of the world today; the threat of terrorism, which is heightening the need for security; the increase of identity crimes, driving the need for security of your electronic identity; the appearance of a global community encouraging world unity; the migration of the financial industry to chip-based technology and the creation of electronic chips that can be implanted in the body to be used for e-commerce, m-commerce and security, you answer the question. If you're not blind or in denial, you will answer yes. Oh, so you say that is opinionated and rude? Not really, it is just direct. We are living in fast-paced times, and there is no time for beating around the bush. If there is an elephant in the room, we need to say "Excuse me, there is an elephant in the room, and I think we should do something about it before it makes a mess on the floor."

The creation of this environment is happening all around us. Trust me when I tell you this, because I am helping to build it during my day job. One of the greatest challenges I had while writing this book was watching the evolution right in front of my eyes. I would see things that I had already written about coming to fruition. I was feeling more like a historian, rather than someone trying to announce what was coming to a neighborhood near you. I would have opportunity to talk about the content of this book, and people would say, "You better hurry up and get it done before it happens." That, of course, made me feel great, as I was struggling to complete the book, writing around a busy work schedule and my commitment to being a good husband and father. I had to pray and beg God constantly to remind me that it was His book, His work, and His announcement. I am just the messenger. He knows the day and the hour.

When I watched the stock market crash and the telecommunications industry fall into crisis, I had to simply rest in the fact that God is sovereign, and the final events needed to launch the return of Jesus will take place when He (God the Father) is ready to begin the final 7 years of judgment on the Earth and not before. Today, He is still choosing to wait, offering man more time to know and receive His Son, Jesus Christ.

As I work, I am watching the convergence of these various technologies into the creation of this electronic ecosystem, creating a global society for communications, finance, and secured electronic identity. Development is happening concurrently all around the world with differing focus but is nonetheless synergistic in a virtual way. All of the actions taken independently in response to market pressure and in leverage of emerged technologies that fuel the release and creation of complementary technologies and services are stepping hand in hand, like a master project plan with dependencies, links, and global resources aiming with deadly focus to create this needed infrastructure to support the events of the end-time theater.

My hope and the purpose of this book is to have you prepared and educated about what is coming so that when you see it happening around you, when you see these technological developments taking place right in front of you, almost daily, that you will ask yourself if you are ready for the return of Jesus Christ to this Earth.

I want you to never look at a swipe reader, a point-of-sale terminal, your TV, your computer, your cell phone, your bankcard or your personal identification in the same way ever again! When you get your new electronic ID card so that you can feel safer in this violent world, or you get your new bankcard with "chip technology" that lets one card "do it all" securely anywhere in the world, or you buy your favorite food from a restaurant, pump gas into your car, or buy a soda from a pop machine, and pay with your handy, dandy "do it all bankcard," think about the plan. When you hear about implant technology being used in the military and government or in medical applications for health reasons or in children or pets so that they can be located if lost or stolen, ask yourself, "Am I ready?"

When you use your cell phone and the GPS chip inside locates where you are, anywhere on the planet, and the phone pops up with a free offer on the display to stop into the coffee shop a few steps ahead because their "loyalty program," integrated with your friendly bank and your new chip card, just identified that you have earned a free "cup of Joe" because you made 10 earlier purchases, ask yourself, "convenience or planned?" When you walk up to a self-service airline-ticketing kiosk at the airport and enter your chip card and it knows everything about your reservation and provides you a boarding pass, or better yet, becomes your "electronic boarding pass," ask yourself, "Is all this security for me?"

When you see the TV looking more like a computer, allowing you to buy dinner, securely on line with just a few clicks of the remote, all from the comfort of your easy chair, remember. You will know when you have "truly arrived" after inserting or even "waving like a magic wand" your new handy, dandy "do it all bankcard" in front of your set top box and poof, just like that, you completed a secure Internet purchase. Before you know it, you will be burning your mouth on hot cheese pizza"—life's good, what more can a person ask for?

I could spend page upon page discussing the various developments that are taking place in the creation of this electronic marketplace, but I am afraid that if I make one more pitch about "e-commerce" this or "m-commerce" that or discuss one more web address or say "Buy it on line at www.xyz" or be connected anytime, anywhere, all the time, you might go into overload. I know I feel that way sometimes, and this is what I have done since 1979 to put food on my table. Rather, **the purpose of this chapter is to get you watching, listening to, and looking at what is happening through new eyes.** It is to help you put some context around all of the craziness. Things are moving at what seems to be light speed, and we are being required to conduct business in ways that are very different from our past perceptions.

I hope you now see that it is not without lasting reason and purpose. Technology exists today to control the buying and selling of goods and services. It simply needs further refinements and expansion around the Earth. Banks can successfully monitor your bank balances and credit lines easily with current technology and deny you a purchase if you are overdrawn or over your credit limit. Basically, they "cut you off," making it impossible to make an electronic purchase. This same technology, when under the control of the Antichrist, along with some new advanced features will give him the power to turn you off, to locate you, and to restrict your ability to buy and sell any goods or services in this new electronic ecosystem.

I assure you as a technologist and a student of prophecy that God's writers foretold something that is not only possible, but has only been made possible in our lifetime. No other time in history could have fulfilled a prophecy like the one described in Revelation, Chapter 13. This makes the imminent reality of the second coming of Jesus Christ even more plausible to consider.

The direction of our walk today is leading us closer and closer to the end of the age, to the fulfillment of the promise made in the Bible thousands of years ago, the promise that Jesus Christ will come again and restore to this Earth the life that He originally intended for us to enjoy. This life includes worshiping Him as God and Creator. It is a life of fulfillment, purpose, joy, peace, no sickness, no pain, no lack of life's basic necessities, no poverty, no conflict, no depression, and basically all the things we have yearned for, because He as Creator placed these yearnings in us while we were yet in our mother's womb.

These very things He intended for us to have and enjoy all along, and because of His true love for us, God gave us each the ability to choose, or what theologians call "free will." Unfortunately, because of Satan's deception of Eve and the free will choice of Adam to disobey the clear instructions of God regarding what they could eat or not eat in the Garden of Eden, Adam and Eve chose sin, disobedience, and separation from God. Man, as a result of this choice, has been suffering from the curse of sin for thousands of years. But, just like the mercy of God shown throughout the scriptures, He always makes a way for us to come back to Him. The way is Jesus Christ! The Bible says, "For there is one God and one mediator between God and men, the man Christ Jesus, who gave himself as a ransom for all men." (1 Timothy 2:5-6).

My prayer is that you will receive him as Lord and Savior today, and that if you know Him personally, you will rededicate your life to him and renew your first love, because He is coming back soon, maybe even tonight. Are you ready, or will He surprise you like a thief in the night?

Chapter Seven

Call To Action

Looking at the World Through New Eyes

Throughout this book, I have reminded you that this is neither a primer on technology nor an exhaustive discussion of any of these technology sectors. Rather, it is a big picture view of technologies, world events, and their interconnections relevant to the preparation of the world for events that will take place in Revelation, Chapter 13.

I have said that <u>A Thief in the Night</u> is evangelistic in nature with its primary focus on creating an awareness of this recently revealed mystery of God for our period in history so as to stir your heart, by this new awareness, to receive Jesus Christ as Savior or to renew your first love for Him if you already have a personal relationship with Jesus as Savior and Lord of your life. Then, with your newfound relationship or renewal of your love for Jesus, you would begin sharing the excitement of His coming with everyone you meet so that they, too, can be ready for the imminent return of Jesus Christ to Earth.

I ask you to set aside your religious, theological positions relevant to end-time events and consider what is going on around you pertaining to the words of Jesus in Matthew 24 and ask yourself if the dissertation reads or sounds like the events of today. Do the leaves on the trees seem to be ripening? There is one clear and undisputed message in all of Christianity, regardless of the denomination: Jesus is coming, and the Bible says he will come as a thief in the night, so we are encouraged to be ready.

I asked you to look at the big picture and to consider if all of this synergistic development and planning was by design. Or do you merely think it is coincidence? I encouraged you to become watchful for these things and to never look at a swipe reader, your computer, a gas pump, your TV, or an ATM machine the same way again. Well, do they look the same? Or have you begun to pick up the paper or a magazine, watched the news, or listen to a broadcast on the radio with an eye on connecting the dots, being aware of the future, asking yourself if you are ready to meet Jesus? I know that since I started preaching this message, and later writing the book, people who have heard the message continually send me updates and articles, and talk about news broadcasts regarding this subject. They are watchful, and this is exciting, because it means that their eyes are on the horizon looking for Jesus to return—and soon!

I hope your answer to this question is that you do believe that this is part of a supernatural plan as predicted in the Bible thousands of years ago, and not coincidence, and that you are now looking at our world through different eyes. If you have not made this connection, then I ask that you pray that

God give you wisdom and reveal the truth of the Bible and the message of Jesus Christ to you. God can use natural revelation, that is the physical beauty and splendor of the Earth, as well, I believe, even the things in our lives such as watching the evolution of technology around the world, to woo us to Him.

Jesus Christ—A Personal God

The real question is: Are you ready to be reconciled to God and receive Jesus Christ into your life? Are you truly searching for answers, for fulfillment in your life? Do you have a place inside that just cannot be filled with anything you do or have—money, friends, mates, clothes, travel, sex, entertainment, religion, or self help. That place inside still remains empty and unfulfilled. Do you continue to search for answers? Do you just try harder or get more of the same to attempt to fill this void to no avail?

Friend, if you are searching, the answer is simple. Each of us is created in the image of God and has a desire to be in relationship, rightly reconciled to our Creator, in relationship with Him because it was His original intent for our lives. He knows us personally, by name, and He fashioned us in our mother's womb. The Bible beautifully describes God the Creator's knowledge and love of you as a person in Psalm 139:

"O LORD, you have searched me and you know me. You know when I sit and when I rise; you perceive my thoughts from afar. You discern my going out and my lying down; you are familiar with all my ways. Before a word is on my tongue you know it completely, O LORD. You hem me in— behind and before; you have laid your hand upon me. Such knowledge is too wonderful for me, too lofty for me to attain. Where can I go from your Spirit? Where can I flee from your presence? If I go up to the heavens, you are there; if I make my bed in the depths, you are there. If I rise on the wings of the dawn, if I settle on the far side of the sea, even there your hand will guide me, your right hand will hold me fast. If I say, "Surely the darkness will hide me and the light become night around me," even the darkness will not be dark to you; the night will shine like the day, for darkness is as light to you. For you created my inmost being; you knit me together in my mother's womb. I praise you because I am fearfully and wonderfully made; your works are wonderful, I know that full well. My frame was not hidden from you when I was made in the secret place. When I was woven together in the depths of the earth, your eyes saw my unformed body. All the days ordained for me were written in your book before one of them came to be. How precious to me are your thoughts, O God! How vast is the sum of them! Were I to count them, they would outnumber the grains of sand. When I awake, I am still with you." (Psalm 139:1-18).

Now, as you read this passage, what does it say to you? Does it speak to a special place inside? Does it touch a spot that has not been touched for a long time or maybe ever? Can you feel the hair on your arms, or the back of your neck, rise up as you hear of the personal love and understanding the Creator has for you? If so, this is the Holy Spirit wooing you, calling to you, loving you, and reaching out to your inner spirit saying that He can fill the emptiness that exists in your life. He can reunite you with your Creator who loves you with an everlasting love.

If you are ready to answer this call and desire to be in relationship with God, it is as simple as receiving a free gift with the simple faith of a child. The gift is eternal life through the sacrificial death of Jesus Christ on the cross and his resurrection from the dead—triumphing over death and sin, making it possible for you to be reconciled to a Holy God and Creator.

Receiving this free gift is easy. The first thing you need to do is acknowledge your need for a Savior, recognize that your sin separates you from God, and confess your sin. The Bible says: "For all have sinned and fall short of the glory of God" (Romans 3:23) and "The wages of sin is death, but the gift of God is eternal life in Christ Jesus our Lord" (Romans 6:23). The Bible also says, "For it is by grace you have been saved, through faith— and this not from yourselves, it is the gift of God— not by works, so that no one can boast" (Ephesians

2:8-9). This means that we are unable, in our own actions or deeds (referred to here as works), to satisfy the requirement of a holy God. Rather it simply requires that you place your faith in Jesus Christ and receive God's unmerited favor or grace. I have heard over the years a neat acronym for the word grace. It is <u>G</u>od's <u>R</u>iches <u>A</u>t <u>C</u>hrist's <u>E</u>xpense (GRACE).

This really says it all: "God demonstrates His own love for us in this: While we were still sinners, Christ died for us" (Romans 5:8). God offers you eternal life (in spite of your sin and the just penalty of death) through the loving sacrifice of Jesus Christ on the cross for your sins. 1 Peter 2:24 says, "He himself (Jesus) bore our sins in his body on the tree, so that we might die to sins and live for righteousness; by his wounds you have been healed." John 3:16 says, "For God so loved the world that He gave His one and only Son, that whoever believes in Him shall not perish but have eternal life. For God did not send His Son into the world to condemn the world, but to save the world through Him. Whoever believes in Him is not condemned, but whoever does not believe stands condemned already because he has not believed in the name of God's one and only Son."

Next the Bible says that we are to believe in our heart and confess with our mouth Jesus Christ. Then we have the assurance of salvation and relationship with God. 1 John 1:9 says: "If we confess our sins, He is faithful and just and will forgive us our sins and purify us from all unrighteousness." Romans 10:9-10 says: "That if you confess with your mouth, "Jesus is Lord," and believe in your heart that God raised him from the dead, you will be saved. For it is with your heart that you believe and are justified, and it is with your mouth that you confess and are saved."

The word of God is clear in showing that first you must believe in your heart, which is faith, and then you are to confess with your mouth, that is to pray and ask Jesus Christ into your life and profess Him publicly as your Savior and Lord. When you do this, you have the promise, based on the truth of the word of God written in the Bible, that you are saved and reunited in relationship to God forever. It is that simple. It is all about Jesus Christ and not about us. He fulfilled every prophecy of the Old Testament. He came to Earth as God in the flesh, lived among men without sin, and submitted Himself to death on the cross to be a sacrifice and fully pay the penalty for sin. He was triumphantly raised from the dead to show mankind that He was victorious over death, and that action sentenced Satan and anyone not believing in Jesus to eternal separation from God.

If you are ready to receive Jesus Christ right now, I ask that you pray the following simple prayer. Based on the promise of the word of God, you can then rest assured in the finished work of Jesus Christ that you are saved and reunited in relationship with God.

God, I know that I am a sinner and that there is nothing I can do to earn eternal life or restore my relationship to you through my works or actions.

God, I believe in my heart that your Son Jesus Christ died for my sins and was raised from the dead and that if I ask Him to forgive me of my sins and restore my relationship with you, that He alone can do this.

Jesus, I ask you now to come into my heart and life and cleanse me from my sin. I desire to receive your gift of eternal life. And through Your loving sacrifice on the cross alone, believe that You will restore my relationship to You and God the Father.

Jesus, I rest in the promise of your written word (the Bible) that I am saved right now because I have believed in my heart and confessed with my mouth that you are my Savior and my Lord. I pray this in the name of Jesus Christ. Amen.

Growth Steps

If you have prayed this prayer, you are now restored to God and have been made part of the family of believers in Jesus Christ all around the world. This is called the church, not a building, but a common family connected together by their central faith in Jesus Christ. You have been, as the Bible declares "reborn" in Jesus Christ or "born again" (John 3:3). As a new believer, you need to begin to do four simple things to grow in your faith and to deepen your relationship with God and Jesus Christ. These four things are not original with me. They are outlined in the Bible and have been recommended by ministries such as the Billy Graham Evangelist Ministry for years as a foundation for your faith and growth.

The four words to remember are:

- Prayer
- Word
- Witnessing
- Church.

Prayer

You need to pray regularly to God. This is how you communicate with God. Remember that He wants to be in relationship with you, so you need to talk to Him. You do this simply, just as you would with someone you love and trust. Prayers can be simple. God, help. God, keep me safe. God, help me know you better. These are all prayers. Then end your prayers "in Jesus' name," because the Bible says that Jesus is our mediator between God and man. Prayer is simply communication with God. Do it often and God will meet you and change your life.

The Apostle Paul said that we are to pray without ceasing, and I believe that this means that God should be part of our daily lives and in our thoughts always. He lives in our hearts, and that means He is with us everywhere we go. Speak with Him regularly, and you will grow in love together!

Word

You need to read the Word (the Bible) as often as you can, because this is one major way that God speaks to you. As you read the Bible, the words will come alive with relevance for today. Start with the Book of John, and then pray that God would lead you to other places in the Bible that will minister to your spirit. Over time, your understanding of the Bible will grow, and it will become more real to you. Another thing I recommend is that you read one chapter of the Proverbs daily. I have read these throughout my Christian life, not always with regularity, but always with timeliness. God always seems to have a message for me on just the right day. There are usually 31 days in the month, so just pick the day and read that chapter. I call it "Proverbs Roulette." The Proverbs will change your life as you begin to internalize the truths of this great book.

Witnessing

We are told that we are to share our faith with others and that our lives are to be light and salt to the Earth (Matthew 28:18-20, 5:13-16). This means that our lives, as we grow in relationship with Jesus, will change, and people will notice.

When they do, you can say, "I am changed because of my relationship with Jesus Christ. He is real to me." This is a witness. We are told that we are to share the good news of the gospel in our neighborhoods and around the world (Acts 1:8). Ask God, when you pray, how you can share your faith, and ask Him to give you opportunities to do so. It will fuel a fire and a passion in your heart that is second to none when you see someone trust in Christ as you have, then become healed and transformed. It is contagious and addictive, and we are to be doing this as part of our daily lives.

Church

You need to attend a church in your local area. Ask God to lead you to a church that will help you grow in your new faith in Him. Find a church that believes and shares the gospel of Jesus Christ. You will find that as you join a church, there are particular things that churches believe called doctrine. Generally the things they believe are written down in what is called a doctrinal statement. Many churches that believe similar things, or have like doctrine, are often grouped together in a denomination such as the Catholics, Methodists, Presbyterians, Baptists, and Lutherans.

The key action, at this time, is to find a church that believes in the gospel of Jesus Christ and is involved in sharing this message in your neighborhood and around the world. My prayer for you is that God will help you find a church so that you can grow in relationship with Him and be in relationship with others who also believe in Jesus Christ. Remember that this is your new family in Christ.

If you have prayed this prayer and have received Jesus Christ into your heart and life, I would like to know. As we further our evangelistic ministry's outreach, we desire to remain a part of your Christian life. Please send a letter or e-mail to the address located in the "Contact the Author" section of the book.

The Bridegroom Is Coming

If you already have a personal relationship with Jesus Christ as Savior and are a member of God's family, then what are you to do with the contents of this book and the message of the urgency of Christ's return to the Earth? Share it with everyone you meet! My hope is that Jesus will not come to your home as a thief in the night, but that you will be like the faithful servant who is about the business of his master, waiting watchfully for his return (Matthew 26:36-51).

Jesus, besides being the head of the church, is also the Bridegroom of the church—hence the church is the Bride of Christ. Remember, as I write here and speak of the "church," I am not speaking about a building or a specific denomination, but rather the universal body of believers who have placed their faith in God and Christ and are redeemed and in restored relation with God the Creator as a result of the work of Jesus Christ on the cross, dying for all of the sins of mankind, past, present, and future.

We are encouraged in the Bible to be ready for the coming of the bridegroom. Matthew 25:1-13 tells the story of the parable of the 10 virgins who were to be prepared and watchful for the coming of the bridegroom. As the parable goes, there were five who were prepared and five who were not. When those who were not prepared heard of the coming of the bridegroom, they were forced to go and get oil for their lamps. During their absence, while they were running this errand, the Bridegroom, Jesus, came, and they missed Him. As a result, they missed out, and Jesus said, "I tell you the truth, I don't know you." (Matthew 25:12).

God is full of grace and mercy. His mercy is new and fresh each morning. He is longsuffering and patient, making a way for each of us to know Him and to walk in His ways. He tells us in His Word that He is coming back, and soon. Be ready! He also gives us the Holy Spirit to dwell inside us to give us the power to do the impossible, which is to live a holy life in a sinful world. He has also blessed us with a commission of sharing the good news of Jesus Christ with our neighborhood, our city, our state, our country, and the world.

What should you do with the contents of this book? Use it as a catalyst to discuss the return of Jesus with people you meet. The Bible is alive and relevant today with prophecy yet to be fulfilled, prophecy that could be fulfilled this very night. We are in the most unique time in the history of mankind. No other time in history have we been so close to the return of our Lord and Savior Jesus Christ. The leaves are ripe unto harvest, and people are asking questions. People are considering their mortality because of events including the September 11, 2001 tragedy, taking place right before their eyes. They are wondering what is happening in the world, as they look at the violence, the moral decay, the lack of absolute truth, and the devaluation of life.

All of these questions create anxiety and uncertainty that can only be answered in the person of Jesus Christ. He can give people the peace they seek and answers to the chaos around them. The Bible encourages us to be ready to give people an answer concerning the good news of Jesus Christ, to basically be ready to represent our faith (1 Peter 3:15). We are ambassadors of Jesus Christ commissioned to share the good news (2 Corinthians 5:20). During such crises of life, people are often trying to make sanity out of insanity. People are searching for relief, for comfort and assurance. You have what they need—Jesus. Only Jesus can provide lasting peace and assurance in the world we live in today. God often uses the crises in people's lives to draw them to Himself, and we need to be ready to share the life-giving message of Jesus Christ.

Sharing the Cure for Life's Ailments

You can, by sharing Jesus with those looking for answers, share the living water of life, which will quench their thirst forever (John 14:4, 6:35). The message of Jesus Christ is relevant and is the medicine needed to heal today's soul longing for answers. If you were a doctor today and created the cure for all types of cancer, simply eradicating this horrible disease with your discovery, what would you do? You would share the news with everyone you know. You would use every possible tool in the modern world to spread the news and distribute this life-giving medicine into the hands of caregivers and patients around the world to cure this ailment and give patients victory over death by cancer.

Well, if you believe in Jesus Christ and have a personal relationship with Him and know that he has changed your life, healed the pains of your heart, healed your physical body, given you the peace of God, and promised that you would **never die** but rather have **eternal life** and dwell with him in a special place prepared for you in Heaven, how much better is this than a temporal cure for cancer?

You have found the cure to eternal death and separation from God in the person of Jesus Christ. He is the living water, and anyone whom you encourage to drink from the well of living water will no longer suffer death but have eternal life. Just think of yourself as a doctor for the soul. You have the medicine that is the cure for all of the problems of mankind today. You simply need to share the good news of the Gospel of Jesus Christ and let the Holy Spirit do His job, which is to convict of sin and woo people to a saving knowledge of Jesus Christ.

But you say, "You don't understand. It's not the same. People are not as excited to hear about the message of Jesus Christ as they would be to hear about the cure for cancer." Well, to that I would say, "You are right," and the reason is simple. People do not understand the finality of the diagnosis of the disease of sin in their life. Satan, in his plan to eternally destroy mankind, has, by the elimination of morality and absolute truth, dummied up sin. People have minimized sin and the consequence of sin, which is physical death, eternal separation from God, and a sentence to Hell to be eternally tormented by fire. The Bible says, "Then death and Hades were thrown into the lake of fire. The lake of fire is the second death. If anyone's name was not found written in the book of life, he was thrown into the lake of fire." (Revelation 21:14-15).

The reason that people you meet don't want to hear the message of Jesus Christ is because, through the power of the Holy Spirit, they are convicted of sin and made accountable for their sin and become aware of their condition. They do not want to believe this condition, but nonetheless, it is true, and it will kill them by eternally separating them from a loving God. It is like the patients who receive the diagnosis for terminal cancer. Their lack of belief or accepting of the diagnosis does not change their condition. They still have cancer and still need a cure.

The cure for "the cancer of sin" is the medicine of Jesus Christ, and with this treatment regime, the patient not only gets healed from the disease, but also gets to drink from the well of living water, giving them eternal life and victory over the worst disease, which is the death of the soul.

So why is it so hard to share such life-changing news, to offer to a dying race the cure for "the cancer of sin"? I am sure that there are many reasons, including our enemy Satan placing a spirit of fear or pride in us, which makes it difficult to share with others. But more simply, I think it is a lack of urgency and an understanding that if people don't receive Jesus Christ today, they are going to suffer the full judgment of a holy and righteous God who will soon be returning to Earth to judge mankind.

My hope, for you that have a relationship with Jesus, is that after reading this book, you will gain a renewed or greater passion for watching for the return of Jesus Christ our Savior, Bridegroom, Lord, King, and Righteous Judge. Jesus is coming, and soon, and says he will come as a thief in the night, surprising many, including His own believers. I hope that the subject content of this book, which is woven into the fabric of your daily life, will prove to be catalyst to stir your heart and give you a hunger to share the message of the imminent return of Jesus with everyone you know or meet. I hope that every time you use a swipe reader or some other electronic portal for purchasing goods and services, you will think of the impending prophecy written in Revelation, Chapter 13. The Bible says that a day is coming when every man rich and poor, slave and free, small and great will be required by the Antichrist to have the mark, which is 666, to be able to buy or sell goods and services (Revelation 13:16). It also says that taking such a mark will seal a person's eternal future and separate him or her from God and sentence him or her to receive the full wrath of God's judgment on mankind (Revelation 14:9-10).

Sharing the Mystery

As we move closer and closer to the fulfillment of this prophecy, you will see this infrastructure emerge before your eyes. And as a result of God revealing this mystery to you in the pages of this book, you are to share this content with others so that He can use the things happening around the world as tools to draw people unto Himself. Some of the joys I had in writing this book were the numerous opportunities I had to share my faith with others as a result of discussing the contents of these pages. I have never had as much opportunity to openly discuss Jesus, even in the workplace, than I have in discussing current technology events and how they relate to end-time prophecy.

People are watching the evolution of technology happening around them, and each has a different view. Some simply are oblivious to what is happening and just see it as life passing by, others see it as "Big Brother" and a threat to their privacy and freedom, some think it is of great convenience, some are fearful of the change but do not know why, some think it will bring about security of identity and finance, and others think it is the devil and evil. Regardless of the view you now have an opportunity to tie these real world events to the Bible in a very real way and use them as a way to share the gospel of Jesus Christ with people you know and meet.

I pray that this vision of things to come will burn in your heart and with each new development make you more passionate about the return of Jesus and the need to share His message in these last days. God says that in the last days He will bring about a great harvest of souls. The Bible says the fields are white unto harvest, but the laborers are few (John 4:35, Matthew 9:37). We need to ask God to give us the boldness and compassion to be part of the great harvest in these last days. Our job is just to go and share. The Holy Spirit will do the work of convicting people of sin and wooing them to Jesus. You just need to show up and offer the cure for sin—a drink of the living water, the medicine of Jesus Christ.

I believe in my heart that the passion of watching for the return of Jesus Christ is contagious. At no other time in the history of mankind have the trees of Matthew, Chapter 24 been so ripe with signs of the return of Jesus Christ. My prayer for you is that Jesus will not come to you as "a thief in the night" but rather find your lamp filled with oil, wick trimmed and light burning, watchfully waiting in anticipation for the glorious return of your Bridegroom, Lord and Savior Jesus Christ! Come quickly, Lord Jesus, your Bride awaits. Amen.

Appendix

Matthew, Chapter 24:3-51

"While Jesus was sitting on the Mount of Olives, the disciples came to him privately and said, "Tell us, when will these things take place, and what will be the sign of your coming and of the end of the age?" Jesus answered them, "See to it that no one deceives you. For many will come in my name and say, 'I am the Christ,' and they will deceive many people. You are going to hear of wars and rumors of wars. See to it that you are not alarmed. These things must take place, but the end hasn't come yet. For nation will rise up in arms against nation, and kingdom against kingdom. There will be famines and earthquakes in various places. But all these things are only the beginning of the birth pains. Then they will hand you over to suffering and will kill you, and you will be hated by all the nations because of my name. Then many people will fall by the way and will betray one another and hate one another. Many false prophets will appear and deceive many people, and because lawlessness will increase, the love of many people will grow cold. But the person who endures to the end will be saved. And this gospel of the kingdom will be proclaimed throughout the world as a testimony to all nations, and then the end will come. So when you see the destructive desecration, mentioned by the prophet Daniel, standing in the Holy Place (let the reader take note), then those who are in Judea must flee to the mountains. The person who is on the housetop must not come down to get what is in his house, and the person who is in the field must not turn back to get his coat. How terrible it will be for women who are pregnant or who are nursing babies in those days! Pray that it may not be in winter or on a Sabbath when you flee. For at that time there will be great suffering, the kind that has not happened from the beginning of the world until now and certainly will never happen again. If those days had not been limited, no life would be saved. But for the sake of the elect, those days will be limited. At that time, if anyone says to you, 'Look! Here is the Christ!' or 'There he is!', don't believe it. For false christs and false prophets will appear and display great signs and wonders to deceive, if possible, even the elect. Remember, I have told you this beforehand. So if they say to you, 'Look! He's in the wilderness,' don't go out looking for him. And if they say, 'Look! He's in the storeroom,' don't believe it. For just as the lightning comes from the east and flashes as far as the west, so will be the coming of the Son of Man. Wherever there's a body, there the vultures will gather. Immediately after the suffering of those days, 'The sun will be darkened, the moon will not give its light, the stars will fall from the sky, and the powers of heaven will be shaken loose.' Then the sign of the Son of Man will appear in the sky, and all the tribes of the earth will mourn when they see 'the Son of Man coming on the clouds of heaven' with power and great glory. He will send out his angels with a loud trumpet blast, and they will gather his elect from the four winds, from one end of heaven to another.

Now learn a lesson from the fig tree. When its branches become tender and it produces leaves, you know that summer is near. In the same way, when you see all these things, you will know that he is near, right at the door. Truly I tell you, this generation will not disappear until these things happen. Heaven and earth will disappear, but my words will never disappear. No one knows when that day or hour will come—not the angels in heaven, nor the Son, but only the Father. For just as it was in the days of Noah, so it will be when the Son of Man comes. In those days before the flood, people were eating and drinking, marrying and giving in marriage right up to the day when Noah went into the ark. They were unaware of what was happening until the flood came and swept all of them away. That's how it will be when the Son of Man comes. At that time two people will be in the field. One will be taken, and the other will be left behind. Two women will be grinding grain at the mill. One will be taken, and the other will be left behind. So keep on watching, because you don't know on what day your Lord is coming. But be sure of this: if the owner of the house had known at what watch of the night the thief was coming, he would have stayed awake and not allowed his house to be broken into. So you, too, must be ready, because at an hour you are not expecting him the Son of Man will come. Who, then, is the faithful and wise servant whom his master has put in charge of his household to give the others their food at the right time? How blessed is that servant whom his master finds doing this when he comes!

Truly I tell you, he will put him in charge of all his property. But if that wicked servant says to himself, 'My master has been delayed,' and begins to beat his fellow servants and eat and drink with the drunks, the master of that servant will come on a day when he doesn't expect him and at an hour that he doesn't know. Then his master will punish him severely and assign him a place with the hypocrites. In that place there will be weeping and gnashing of teeth."

About The Author

Lee Kedrie is a husband and father of four children and started his career in telecommunications in 1979. Lee opened his first technology business in 1983 and quickly developed a reputation of being a Convergence Architect. His vision to converge telecommunications and computing technologies together to impact employee productivity and a company's revenues has now become a common industry practice. During Lee's entrepreneurial years he designed and installed technology solutions in the US and internationally and achieved top dealer ranking.

In 2001 Lee Kedrie retired from the world of self employment after a successful merger in 1999 with Certus Corporation for the pursuit of greater family relationship and ministry opportunities. He joined a Fortune 10 technology company and is a Master Technologist serving as a Solutions Architect and Evangelist to the top corporations in the world designing and deploying next generation technology and infrastructure solutions.

Lee is a requested and entertaining public speaker and regularly speaks in the US and internationally on convergence, next generation technology and infrastructure strategies and IT consolidation. He also teaches on healing and deliverance and the return of Jesus Christ in local churches and group settings.

Lee and his wife are also active in the evangelism of hearts toward Jesus Christ. As co-pastors in the healing and deliverance ministry they have witnessed the personal touch of Jesus on many lives and have seen the healing of bodies, souls and spirits. This passion for personal relationship with Jesus Christ is at the foundation of their marriage and family. Both Lee and his wife believe the return of Jesus Christ is imminent and they desire to share the personal, life changing, love of Jesus with everyone they meet.

Lee Kedrie is a converted Moslem and was called to itinerate evangelism as a youth. His deepest desire is to see people experience the joy of a personal relationship with Jesus Christ. He hopes after reading a Thief in the Night you will never look at technology the same again and that these pages will catalyze the question in your mind—"Am I ready for the return of Jesus, or will he surprise me like a thief in the night"?

Contact the Author

Please write or e-mail us if you have placed your trust in Jesus Christ as a result of reading the message God has revealed in these pages.

Please contact us regarding opportunities to share this content and the gospel of Jesus Christ with your community. It is my calling, as Steward of this common day mystery, which God revealed for these last days, to share this message and preach the gospel of Jesus Christ to all peoples of the Earth for His glory and purposes!

Letters: Lee Kedrie, C/O English Channel Press, P.O. Box 461174, Aurora, Colorado, 80046-1174

E-mail: lee.kedrie@englishchannelpress.com

Speaking requests: Please request on line at www.englishchannelpress.com and check the event calendar for scheduled events near you or call us at 303-699-3383.

"I became a servant of this gospel by the gift of God's grace given me through the working of his power. Although I am less than the least of all God's people, this grace was given me: to preach to the Gentiles the unsearchable riches of Christ, and to make plain to everyone the administration of this mystery, which for ages past was kept hidden in God, who created all things. His intent was that now, through the church, the manifold wisdom of

God should be made known to the rulers and authorities in the heavenly realms, according to his eternal purpose which he accomplished in Christ Jesus our Lord." (Ephesians 3:7-10)

"In the last days, God says, I will pour out my Spirit on all people. Your sons and daughters will prophesy, your young men will see visions, your old men will dream dreams. Even on my servants, both men and women, I will pour out my Spirit in those days, and they will prophesy. I will show wonders in the heaven above and signs on the earth below, blood and fire and billows of smoke. The sun will be turned to darkness and the moon to blood before the coming of the great and glorious day of the Lord. And everyone who calls on the name of the Lord will be saved." (Acts 2:17-21 and Joel 2:28-32a)

"The great day of the Lord is near—near and coming quickly. Listen!" (Zephaniah 1:14)

Give the gift of *A Thief in the Night* to your family, friends, colleagues, pastors and church leaders

Order here or on line at
www.englishchannelpress.com

☐ Yes. I want _____ copies of A Thief in the Night for $16.95 each. (Complete address form on back of page)

☐ Yes. I want to be notified when Lee Kedrie publishes any new books or articles.

☐ Yes. I am interested in having Lee Kedrie speak or give a seminar to my church, company, school, association or organization. Please send me information.

Include $3.95 shipping and handling for one book, and $1.95 for each additional book. Colorado residents must include applicable sales tax and Canadian orders must include payment in US funds. Call for bulk discounts.

Payment must accompany orders. Allow 3 weeks for delivery.

My check or money order for $_____ is enclosed.

Please charge my ☐ Visa ☐ MasterCard ☐ American Express

Call (303) 699-3383

Make your check payable and return to

English Channel Press
P.O. Box 461174
Aurora, Colorado 80046-1174

www.englishchannelpress.com
Fax: (303) 693-2797

Please provide your credit card and mailing information to complete your order

Name _____

Organization _____

Address _____

City/State/Zip _____

Phone _____

E-mail _____

Card # _____

Exp. Date _____

Signature _____

Thank you for your order

English Channel Press

www.englishchannelpress.com